Does the Bible teach pacifism?

R. E. D. Clark

Marshalls
Fellowship of Reconciliation

Marshalls Paperbacks
Marshall Morgan & Scott
1 Bath Street, London EC1V 9LB

Copyright © R. E. D. Clark 1976, 1983

First published in 1976 by the Fellowship of Reconciliation

This revised edition published 1983 by Marshall Morgan &
Scott and the Fellowship of Reconciliation

ISBN: 0 551 00970 5

Typeset by Preface Ltd, Salisbury, Wilts.
Printed in Great Britain by
Hazell Watson & Viney Ltd, Aylesbury, Bucks

Dedicated

to the flock of Christ's sheep, in the hope that they will not sharpen their teeth and claws to keep the wolves at bay.

Contents

Foreword

KNOWING THAT THIS was a book on pacifism, I was not sure whether I could honestly write a foreword to it. I have up to now thought that the pacifist position could not claim full support from the Bible, but I have found Dr. Clark very convincing. He has had a fresh look at what the Old Testament actually says about war and violence, and he draws very strong support, as one expects, from the teaching of Jesus Christ. He deals with the passages that are used to justify war, and he draws a sensible parallel between the attitudes to slavery and to war.

If one admits ambiguity in any line of New Testament teaching, it is always right to look at the interpretation taken by the early Christians in post-biblical times, and this book sets out emphatic evidence for their pacifist position, which presumably they had inherited from apostolic times, and hence from Jesus Christ himself.

If all this were not enough, this book gives terrifying outlines of what has happened since Christians followed the standards of the world in making war. There is a particularly relevant section on Christian involvement with revolution and violence.

If other Christians find this book as convincing as I have done I shall be all the more grateful for being allowed to write this foreword for one whose wisdom I have admired and whose friendship I have valued since Cambridge days.

J. Stafford Wright,
Bristol

Preface

LET IT BE STATED clearly at the outset that this book has been written by one who accepts the Bible, rather than the church, the example set by Christian leaders, or even the 'inner light' of conscience, as the final authority in the Christian life. He believes, that if words mean anything the New Testament teaches quite plainly that on the last day, the words and teaching of Jesus will constitute the standard by which men will be judged. For each one, said Jesus, 'The word that I have spoken will be his judge on the last day' (Jn. 12:48). 'Heaven and earth will pass away but my words shall not pass away' (Mk. 13:31). The man who knows what Jesus commanded and does it is likened in the gospel to a wise man who builds his house on rock; the man who knows but fails to do is likened to one who builds on sand (Mt. 7:24f).

This book is about violence – about war and the use of force. Today more than ever before, perhaps, we need to know what Jesus and the Bible generally has to say on this subject. In the pages that follow this is what we shall be attempting to find out.

The Bible is a book which needs to be used carefully; the story of the temptation in the wilderness reminds us that even the devil can quote Scripture to his own advantage.

How we interpret the Bible is therefore our responsibility. Through perversity, laziness or ignorance (which is no excuse if we are content to remain ignorant!) men, like the devil, often prefer interpretations which are plainly false. Sometimes, too, they are silly. (The author well remembers a conversation with a fellow undergraduate who thought that Jesus had taught his disciples that they were fools and slow of heart to believe what the prophets had written! See Lk. 24:25 in AV.) Often we badly need the correction and advice of fellow Christians but the Bible still provides the final standard both for them and us.

Having made clear what our starting point is to be, let us put the question: Is it right, in a just cause, to take up arms whether in an old-fashioned national war or in one of the newer ideological civil wars? When evil men flourish, when the national enemy in time of war, or the civil authority in time of peace, is responsible for perpetrating injustice, when peaceful methods of persuasion fail, where does Christian duty lie?

Quite likely, after a short discussion with Christian friends, we shall come to the conclusion that there is nothing in the Bible to tell us that we should not fight in a good cause. Indeed, on occasion, this may appear the honourable and right thing to do.

The reasons given for this decision will probably run something like this.

There are many instances in the Old Testament where God's people were told to fight the Lord's battles against the ungodly heathen. Though the New Testament tells Christians to be merciful, kind and loving, we reflect that for a Christian, if not for others, it ought to be possible to love someone you are fighting: certainly in a traditional war you would want to rescue him, perhaps risking your life in doing so, if he were wounded. If he was your prisoner you would feed and clothe him. War is a terrible thing, but so is surgery, yet we all know that the best way a doctor can love his fellow man is sometimes to cut him with a knife. May not the same principle at times apply to the body politic? Looked at in this way the Golden Rule that we should do to others as we should like them to do to us does not seem incompatible with fighting them in time of war.

In the New Testament the AV gives the impression that Jesus drove the money changers out of his Father's house with a whip: was not that a violent action? On one occasion he even told his disciples to sell a cloak to buy a sword. John the Baptist preached to the soldiers telling them to be fair and considerate to the people and not to go on strike for higher pay, but he did not tell them to leave the army. St. Paul says that Christians should obey the powers that be, because they are ordained of God and, in time of war if not of civil strife, the state commands service with the armed forces. Then again the military metaphor is often used of the Christian life: St. Paul would certainly have approved of the hymn 'Onward Christian soldiers', but hardly of one beginning 'Onward Christian adulterers'! Added to all this, as everybody knows, many fine Christian men have served and still serve in the armed forces of their respective countries and nearly all major branches of the Christian church teach that it is right for them to do so.

And so, putting all the evidence together, it is surely right, at least when the State so commands, for Bible-loving Christians to fulfil their duty to their country by taking up arms in a good cause.

This at least is how many sincere Christians argue. Are they right? In the pages which follow we shall discuss the arguments carefully together with others, some of which are often overlooked. We shall see that the question will then appear in a very different light.

1:
The slippery slope to total war

IT IS USUAL for Christians to teach their children that one sin leads to another; that once we start upon a downward path it is difficult to stop. In the language of the Victorians: 'Sow a thought, reap an action; sow an action, reap a habit; sow a habit, reap a destiny'.

Few people, however, think of this in relation to the history of the church. In this chapter we shall be thinking especially of the use of weapons in warfare.

All down history, as new and more deadly weapons came to be used in war, they were usually denounced by Christians. This happened long before the development of modern warfare. Thus the crossbow, which gradually replaced the short bow from around the 10th century, was formally condemned by the second Lateran Council in 1139 AD.

In the middle ages the Turks started to use pyrotechnic compositions in their battles with Christians. This use of fire was condemned by Christendom as outrageous, barbaric and satanic. (This was hardly consistent, perhaps, seeing that the Christian Byzantine Empire, centred in Constantinople, had protected itself from attack by the use of Greek Fire, probably burning oil projected at the enemy by means of a pump, for centuries.)

Gunpowder was invented by the Chinese around 1000 AD and the discovery was quickly followed, within a century, by 'a vigorous development of explosive weapons' (Needham) but peaceful uses (other than for entertainment) were hardly at all developed. There is very little evidence of its use in blasting. For two centuries weapons based on gunpowder were used on a grand scale in China, producing devastation and fearful suffering among the Chinese while the power groups fought for supremacy.

Those who are disposed to criticise Christianity for the inconsistency of Christians should reflect that in China gunpowder was no sooner discovered than it was used in war without moral scruple, and not gunpowder only but effective poison 'gas' too (arsenical and mercurial minerals in pyrotechnic compositions). In the West, on the other hand, the influence of Christianity long acted as a buffer, holding back development of new scientific weapons for centuries. No other religion appears to have influenced mankind in this way.

When at last knowledge of gunpowder reached the Western world in the 12th century it was felt by many that even the wickedest of men could not have sunk so low as to produce such a terrible material. The invention was the work of the devil who communicated the secret to mankind. The secret lies in the very large proportion of saltpetre (75%) which

16

gunpowder contains: an early woodcut depicts the devil jogging the arm of one of the supposed discoverers (Schwartz) while he is weighing out this ingredient. Even saltpetre (potassium nitrate) itself seemed tainted with evil. Shakespeare calls it the 'villainous saltpetre' while according to one early author it is formed in nature 'out of the Saltness of the Earth where Beasts and Men have promiscuously mingled' (Leonardus, *The Mirror of Stones*, 1750 Eng. Ed. p. 211).

That there was something wrong in a Christian making gunpowder for war is an idea which lingered on for centuries. Thus Richard Watson (1737–1816), one time Professor of Chemistry in Cambridge and later Bishop of Llandaff, discovered a method for improving the charcoal used in its manufacture: his method saved England a great deal of money around the turn of the century. Addressing himself to King George III the Bishop stated, 'I ought to be ashamed of myself inasmuch as it is a scandal in a Christian bishop to instruct men in the mode of destroying mankind' (*Anecdotes in the Life of Richard Watson*, 1818, p. 243).

The discovery of gunpowder in the West led eventually to the manufacture of guns. (The Chinese had had them since the early 13th century). Their use in war was quickly felt to be unchristian. An early woodcut (15th cent.) shows a devil pointing a gun at the risen Christ. 'Christians do invade Christians with the weapons of hell' cries Erasmus, 'who can believe that guns were the invention of men?' The new invention took heroism out of war. The brave knight looked to God to help him punish the evil doer, but now the veriest scoundrel might shoot down the brave knight at a safe distance without so much as risking his skin. When such things could happen the idea of a just war was beginning to lose meaning.

With the invention of the Maxim gun in recent times it seemed as if the last traces of humanitarianism in war had been destroyed. It is 'the most terrible arm yet invented . . . it is frightful, five or six men armed with such a weapon could destroy a whole regiment in a few minutes', is how a contemporary Christian writer described it in 1870, believing that the invention presaged Daniel's 'time of trouble such as never was since there was a nation', when evil would be triumphant over the world (J. Cumming, *The Seventh Vial*, 1870, p. 34).

With each new invention over the centuries Christians protested. Their protests were often effective for a time, but gradually the new weapons came to be accepted as a matter of course. Both Maxim and Nobel were motivated by the thought that if only they could make a weapon sufficiently terrible, no human being would risk using it and wars would cease. It appears that for a time both thought they had succeeded but in fact wars, when they came, were only made more destructive than before. To anticipate, the advent of the atomic bomb in our day would appear to have realised their dreams, for nuclear explosions are vastly more destructive than machine guns and dynamite. Temporally, at least, these too have given us a kind of peace, yet Kitson reckons that the fear of atomic weapons has served to help subversion and insurgency throughout the world ever since (F. Kitson, *Low Intensity Operations*, 1971).

Coming to World War 1 we are struck by the way in which, though at first the new developments in war caused disgust, they soon came to be accepted as common place.

Serious bombing of the civilian population in England started in the Summer of 1917 and on June 18 an entire class of 16 children most of them under 6, was killed in a London school. The press carried some violent demands for retaliation but in the House of Lords Viscount Knutsford said he could not 'believe that any man who had seen women and children injured and torn to pieces, as he had, would ever dare to say that England should be guilty of such a crime' – a remark greeted with applause. The Earl of Derby, replying for the government, was likewise cheered when he said, 'The idea of an eye for an eye in the way of massacring women and children was absolutely repugnant to the nation' (*Hansard* and *Times* of 27 June). A semi-official telegram sent from Amsterdam, recorded that 'the grief in Germany is not less than the grief in Great Britain', while no one (no newspaper?) in Germany even suggested that civilian killings in England should be regarded as a reprisal for Germans killed in Allied raids on Karlsruhr, Freiburg and Trier (*Times*, 29 June).

As World War 1 progressed less and less sympathy was felt for civilians who were forced to suffer. The wicked enemy had to be defeated at all costs, even by starvation as in the Allied blockade, and morals took a second place. Christians who, at the beginning, would have been scandalised by lies in high places, accepted, quite uncritically, the outpourings of the propaganda machine. An entire department operated in France to fake photographs of German atrocities while the rumour was spread abroad that the Germans were using dead bodies to make soap and lubricants for guns, stories well calculated to inflame Hindus against Germany. The full story was later published by Lord Ponsonby (*Falsehood in War Time*, 1928).

Meanwhile, everywhere, in the non-Christian world, the fact that Christian nations could fight to the death was a cause of scandal. Albert Schweitzer was told by an African savage that Europeans kill each other 'merely out of cruelty, because of course they don't want to eat the dead' (Schweitzer, *My Life and Thought*, 1933, p. 172). Malinowski recounted the story of a Trobriander who was told about the number of corpses after a single battle near Verdun. At first he was incredulous, for it was quite impossible for people to eat so much flesh. Then he burst into indignation: 'Is it not a shame to kill so many people for no use?' he asked. (Quoted, M. Ossowska, *Social Determinants of Moral Ideas*, 1971, p. 109.)

Other methods of warfare followed the same pattern. The invention and use of submarines, the sinking of merchant ships on the high seas, the use of flame throwers and above all of poison gas were deemed criminal at the start of the war, but gradually came to be accepted by both sides as a matter of course.

The use of poison gas in warfare had often been suggested in the 19th century but rejected on Christian and humanitarian grounds. In 1853, at the time of the Crimean war, Sir John Playfair wrote to the Government suggesting the use of brittle tubes containing yellow phosphorus in carbon disulphide with the addition of a little beeswax or petroleum, for use as incendiaries. He also suggested that shells should be filled with the arsenical compound cacodyl cyanide to produce poisonous vapour. Both suggestions were rejected. In 1855 Lord Dondonald proposed that burning sulphur should be used at the seige of Sebastopol: again the idea was rejected. At The Hague Peace Conference in 1899 the Powers pledged themselves not to use noxious vapours in war. The use of an explosive (ammonium perchlorate) which liberated chlorine seems to have given the German high command an excuse to use this gas in 1915 after which both sides used it and other poisons (notably phosgene and mustard gas) on an increasing scale. Fortunately gas was not used in World War 2 but the reason lay not in Christianity now, but in its relative ineffectiveness under battle conditions, coupled with the fear of retaliation and the unknown hazards of advancing into a gassed area. Chemical weapons of many kinds were used in the Vietnam war, as was gas in several minor wars. More recently (1980 and 1981) repeated claims have been made that it is being or has been used in various places. Considerable stocks of chemical weapons are kept in America and in the USSR. These include nerve gases (or compounds which

21

react to give nerve gases when mixed just before use – the so-called 'binary weapons'). One chemical called BZ which causes mental disorientation and is said to be 100 times as potent as LSD, came into the news when it was revealed that storage tanks containing it had leaked in America on five occasions (*Daily Telegraph*, 25 July, 1979). Several MPs have said that an initial chemical attack on Britain is more probable than a nuclear attack (*Times*, 2 July, 1980) and there has been agitation for the production of chemical counter weapons. These developments are now discussed in a matter-of-fact way that would have horrified our Christian ancestors.

At the start of World War 2 the Germans obliterated large areas of Warsaw and Rotterdam. It was agreed in England that governments in time of war had no right to kill women and children or to destroy their homes, just because they chanced to live in a town where munition factories were located. Accordingly, the Allies developed 'pin-point' bombing, but by the end of the war it had been replaced by 'obliteration' or 'area' bombing. The climate of opinion changed rapidly as the war progressed and those who had said that they would never support a war which involved ruthless methods made possible by modern technology, forgot what they had said only a year or so before. Thus one leading editor started by saying, 'The deliberate killing of the non-violent is murder. If war degenerated into wilful slaughter of the innocent, Christians must either become pacifists or give up their religion' (*Christian News Letter*, October 1940). By July 1943 the same writer in the same

22

journal said, 'It is the acceptance of war that increasingly seems to me to be the fundamental issue, while the precise point where the line is to be drawn is of secondary importance . . . If you accept war, military necessity in so far as it is a real necessity, must prevail'.

David Irving (*The Destruction of Dresden*, 1963 and later editions) and Martin Middlebrook (*The Nuremberg Raid; The Battle of Hamburg*, 1980) have researched into how the bombing raids on German cities were conducted by the Royal Air Force from 1943 onwards. It transpires that about half (49%) of the British effort was devoted to the night bombing of towns. The horrors caused by the resulting firestorms are unimaginable. On one night in Hamburg in 1943 40,000 were killed: only the civilian part of the city, that North of the Elbe, was attacked. In Dresden 100,000 were killed in one night. In the cities all the men of fighting age had been called up, so that only old people, women and children were left, while schoolboys often manned the guns. One lady tried to find her parents after the firestorm at Hamburg. 'How terribly must these people have died' she wrote. 'The smallest children lay like fried eels on the pavement. Even in death they showed sign of how they must have suffered – their hands and arms stretched out as if to protect them from the pitiless heat.' Later, a member of one RAF crew said: 'Whatever statesmen and braided air marshalls may say and write, it was barbarous in the extreme. "Whoever harms a hair of one of these little ones . . . " I expect no mercy in the life to come. The Teacher told us clearly. We disobeyed'

23

(Middlebrook on Hamburg, pp. 276, 349).

By this time the church had become quite ineffective. Bishop Barnes of Birmingham who had long been a pacifist protested. George Bell, Bishop of Chichester, who was not a pacifist, protested also but was violently attacked by the press for so doing. It was feared that he might undermine the morale of the air crews. Later his stand during the war prevented his election to the Archbishopric of Canterbury, or so it was widely believed. Otherwise there was little opposition to the bombing from the church – Bell received no support from Archbishop Temple.

In Europe the American bombers attacked military targets only and in daylight so that they could see what they were doing. But this did not apply to Japan where firebombs were rained on Tokyo and where, later, the dropping of the first atom bombs caused an outburst of indignation and horror – particularly in view of what might be in store for the human race – but little sense of shame. After the war it was common for Germans to say that they were not too upset by the crimes which their countrymen had committed, for they could see little to choose, morally, between these and what the Allies had done in Japan.

Today, as Nicholas Humphrey reminds us: 'The world had come a long way between 1939 and 1945. It has come far further between 1945 and 1981. There are today in readiness for military use not two but 50,000 nuclear weapons' (Bronowski Lecture, *The Listener*, 29 October 1981). 'We are rushing headlong towards a precipice' said Lord Mountbatten not long before his death, but there is no one 'to reach for the brakes.' Many Christians, like many non-Christians, approve the atomic deterrent. They realise the danger but think the risk worth while.

The lesson we may draw from history is that, having once made a compromise with war, Christians in every age have tried to set a limit to what a Christian may do. But to no avail. Each generation is horrified by new applications of science and technology applied to war, but takes for granted the things that horrified the generation before. Once the Golden Rule is abandoned there is no resting place and, in war time, especially, the slide is very rapid. The methods of modern warfare would have horrified the Neros and Ivans of the past but in our day we – Christians with the rest – are only too apt to take them for granted.

2:
How people persuade themselves that wrong is right

SINCE THE DAWN of history people have held widely different opinions about all manner of things. Yet on reading the Christian Scriptures an outsider might be entitled to think that among Christians, at all events, there ought to be a large measure of agreement, at least on important practical issues. Jesus prayed that his disciples might be one; his church is spoken of as like a body and a body will hardly function at all unless its parts are coordinated, working smoothly together (1 Cor. 12). Sects and divisions are roundly condemned (1 Cor. 1:10f; Gal. 5:20 etc) and at the end of the New Testament the united body of faithful Christians appears as the Lamb's wife in the heavenly Jerusalem. Not much scope for division, one might think.

Yet in fact as we all know there is a wide spectrum of opinions among Christians. They differ about politics, about the authority of the church and of priests, about how worship should be conducted, about baptism, about capital punishment, and a great deal else beside. In particular they differ about war.

To a large extent the upbringing and education of children must take the blame. When very young we do not think things out for ourselves; for the most part we accept blindly the opinions and values of our elders. Early thought-habits tend to persist through life unless they receive hard knocks to change them. So of course we have our differences.

But we cannot leave the question here. If our Christianity is sincere, we shall certainly want to know and do what is right. What are the dangers which may lead us astray? In this chapter we shall consider three of them, especially in the light of biblical teaching. They are:

1   The failure of conscience to work properly.
2   The fear which kills love.
3   The belief that some people are sub-human.

1   *The numbing of conscience*
All Christians believe that conscience is a God-given gift to warn us when we take the wrong path. Yet contrary to expectation conscience often seems a poor guide, even in the life of the Christian. It is most needed when prejudice and tradition lead men astray yet here, for some reason, it seems strangely ineffective. So we had better start by asking what Christianity teaches about conscience.

All branches of the Christian church recognise that conscience is not an infallible guide to what is right and wrong. They recognise that conscience can slumber, can be distorted or can disappear altogether. It cannot, without qualification, be called the voice of God.

In the New Testament we find the subject broached on a number of occasions. Jesus said that the time would come when the very murderers of his disciples would think they were doing God's will (Jn. 16:2). In the day of judgment, he said, many who thought they had lived good lives will be startled to be told that they were workers of iniquity (Mt. 7:23; 25:44).

St. Paul speaks of consciences which are 'seared' (1 Tim. 4:2), 'corrupted' (Titus 1:15) or just weak (1 Cor. 8:7) and in many other passages it is implied that even in the converted Christian conscience does not always work properly. Paul, honest man that he was, was never quite sure that his own conscience was 100% reliable. 'I am not aware of anything against myself, but I am not thereby acquitted', he said (1 Cor. 4:4). This is a doubt we must all share.

Conscience is easily distorted or killed if we take too much notice of what other people say and do. So the Christian is told that he must on no account follow the example of those around him regardless of whether it is right or wrong. 'Do not be conformed to this world' says St. Paul, but 'prove (test) what is the will of God, what is good and acceptable' (Rom. 12:2). People who 'measure themselves with one another' he says, 'are without understanding' (2 Cor. 10:12). As Christians we must not act 'to please men, but to please God who tests our hearts' (1 Thess. 2:4). In the New Testament the men-pleasers are the scribes and Pharisees who seek prestige and worldly honour rather than the praise that comes from God (Jn. 5:44 etc.). Christians are not to be like them.

This teaching is basic to the New Testament. The Christian must witness to Christ, prepared for ridicule and persecution, just because his standards are not those of the world.

In our day most people, though they give lip service to this teaching of the New Testament, disregard it when it comes to the point. They compete with one another for better cars, houses, furniture, jewellery and clothes in order to keep up with the Jones's. On every hand we see how society is organised so that people will do what is expected of them without question. Conscience, instead of being exercised by the Christian gospel, goes to sleep and many of us, though Christians, become conformed to the world before realising what is happening.

Is the readiness with which Christians are prepared to resort to violence another instance of the slumber of conscience? Though we have said nothing to suggest it, this is at least a possibility.

Let us end this section with a few examples to show how easily conscience is stifled.

For most of his life Archbishop Cranmer accepted the common opinion that 'all Christian princes have committed unto them the whole cure of all their subjects' who are bound to obey in religious matters as well as in secular. As a result when Mary came to the throne Cranmer recanted the views he had been preaching for years. Only later did he see that the doctrine of the divine right of kings could not be carried thus far and that it was his duty to preach what he knew was true rather than to obey the Queen – for which opinion he was burnt at Oxford.

The man who is unrepentant when he has stolen small things will find his conscience in a very sleepy state when he steals on a larger scale. 'He who is faithful in a very little is faithful also in much; and he who is dishonest in a very little is dishonest also in much' (Lk. 16:10) said Jesus.

Autobiographies of criminals bear this out. For A.K. Munro (*Autobiography of a Thief*, 1972) it was the unauthorized borrowing of a motor cycle, followed by thefts of small quantities of petrol to make it seem that the vehicle had not been used, which led to theft as a career.

Douglas Curtis (*From Dartmoor to Cambridge*, 1973) says that 'the thought of stealing had filled me with revulsion'; but after he had started to steal, starting in a small way, ' . . . in a few short months stealing had become as familiar to me as breathing'.

Otto Hahn, the scientist, had a Christian upbringing and wrestled with Christian problems for much of his life. Though in the end he could no longer accept the 'living God' of the Bible, the Bible always moved him as did no other book.

In World War 1 Hahn, in common with nearly all the well-known German chemists of the day, was caught up with the manufacture and use of poison gas. 'I threw myself into the work wholeheartedly' he says. 'As a result of continuous work with these highly toxic substances our minds were so numbed that we no longer had any scruples about the whole thing.' On the Russian front, after he had discharged chlorine and phosgene, Hahn visited the trenches ahead. 'I felt profoundly ashamed . . . First we attacked the Russian soldiers with our gases, and then when we saw the poor fellows lying there, dying slowly, we tried to make breathing easier for them by using our own life-saving devices on them. It made us realise the utter senselessness of war. First you do your utmost to finish off the stranger over there in the enemy trench, and then when you're face to face with him you can't bear the sight of what you've done and you try to help him. But we couldn't save those poor fellows' (*My Life*, 1970, pp. 122, 132).

As Hahn and many others point out, modern war (including civil war) is made easier because men do not see what they do. Shells, napalm, mines, bombs, like poison gas, are made to function by pressing buttons, manipulating switches, pulling triggers, setting time fuses or turning cocks. Those who do these things are shielded from the sight of the death agonies of those they kill, the tears of widows, or the plight of the fatherless.

Sometimes conscience dies altogether. The world was scandalized by the utter indifference shown by Charles Manson and his girl associates in the Californian desert (1968–9) to the suffering they caused.

Hitler's Germany afforded classical examples of this. When the former war criminals faced Allied justice at Nürnberg it soon became apparent that few of them thought they had done anything wrong.

Of one Jew-baiting murderer a psychologist concluded that 'he had not the slightest consciousness of guilt; even the idea that he had committed a punishable offence was entirely alien to him'. Of Hoess, described as the greatest murderer of all time, who was responsible for the death of three million people, it is said that 'of any sense of guilt there was no sign, for the only thing he knew was that he had done what was right'. Speaking of this man's trial Gilbert remarks: 'There was no indication of emotional reaction of any sort as he calmly related how he had received and executed Himmler's orders to exterminate Jewish families by the trainload.' 'I am entirely normal' said Hoess, 'even while I was doing this extermination work, I led a normal family life.' When Hoess was asked whether he 'thought the Jews deserved such a fate' he said that such a question 'never even occurred to us' and, later, 'the thought of disobeying an order would simply never have occurred to anybody and somebody else would have done just as well if I hadn't . . . ' (*Rudolph Hoess, Commandant of Auschwitz*, 1959). No doubt the Commandant of Andersonville, the Russians at Katyn and the Americans at My Lai thought the same.

It is very sad to reflect that Hoess had been brought up as a Christian (Roman Catholic): at one point it was even his ambition to become a Christian missionary for he was deeply impressed by the work of the White Fathers in Africa. When looking for a job he drifted into the SS with no conception of what was involved.

To bring the story up to date, Stanley Milgram

has described experiments which show that quite ordinary people rarely bother about conscience at all, provided they can throw responsibility on somebody else. Milgram's subjects were told that they were helping in an experiment to find out if punishment is an aid to learning. When the people they were supposed to be teaching failed to remember what they were told, they were punished by electric shocks. (In fact, the supposed learners were actors who only pretended to suffer.) Most of the subjects were prepared to cause any amount of suffering, even to the point of death, yet with no trace of hatred or sadism. When they asked if such suffering was necessary, they were simply told that 'the experiment requires you to continue', or, 'it is absolutely essential that you continue' which proved sufficient to allay the twinges of conscience. There is 'something far more dangerous' than anger or hatred, says Milgram, it is 'the capacity for man to abandon his humanity . . . as he merges his unique personality into larger institutional structures'. 'A substantial proportion of people do what they are told to do irrespective of the content of the act and without limitations of conscience, so long as they perceive that the command comes from a legitimate authority' (S. Milgram, *Obedience to Authority*, 1974).

These are terrible examples of the death of conscience. But no Christian can afford to be complacent. We shall see in the sequel that men acknowledged by all as devout Christians have not infrequently allowed blind spots to develop in their minds with the result that they acted criminally.

We must not be disillusioned by this for the Bible warns us that this can happen. In the Old Testament Abraham's behaviour was not always exemplary. David, the 'man after God's own heart' once committed adultery followed by murder. In the New Testament Peter denied his Lord with an oath while the other disciples forsook their Master and fled. David seems to have been untroubled by conscience until Nathan visited him (2 Sam. 12); and Peter, too, until he heard the cock crow.

These examples show how easily we may fall, and how wrong it can be to copy blindly what other people do. This undermines the argument that because so-and-so was a Christian under arms, fighting cannot be wrong. To know if it is wrong we must examine the Scriptures and our own consciences. Even when we see our way clearly, however, we must be careful not to judge others. As St. Paul puts it: 'Who are you to pass judgment on the servant of another? It is before his own master that he stands or falls' (Rom. 14:4).

Finally, the obvious sinfulness of some Christians often leads atheists and others to argue that Christianity does not improve man's morals. This, of course, is grossly unfair, for Christianity *does* implant seeds in the minds of men which, when they have grown, enable them to see the wickedness of commonly accepted standards of conduct. As a result vast social benefits have accrued to mankind. It is no criticism of seeds that they do not grow instantaneously, or that they sometimes fail to germinate.

2 *Too frightened to love: the witchcraft story*

A second reason why people sometimes do what otherwise they would know to be wrong is because they are afraid. No doubt Peter, in denying his Lord, was fearful lest, as a disciple of Jesus, he too would be tried and condemned. For a little while the sheer terror of such an outcome made all thought of loyalty pale into insignificance.

In English as in Greek the verb 'to fear' has two distinct meanings. It can mean either 'to feel or show respect for' (as in 'fear God') *or* 'to be in terror or dread of'. In this second sense of terror or dread, fear of man is condemned in no uncertain terms in the New Testament.

Briefly, the New Testament teaches that we must trust God for the provision of our needs, an attitude of fearful foreboding as to what the future may bring being displeasing to God who is our Father (Mt. 6:25–34). Jesus said 'Let not your hearts be troubled, neither let them be afraid' (Jn. 14:27). Christ's purpose was 'to deliver all those who through fear of death were subject to lifelong bondage' (Heb. 2:15). The Christian who abides in the love of God has confidence in the day of judgment because 'there is no fear in love, but perfect love casts out fear . . . he who fears is not made perfect in love' (1 Jn. 4:18). It is the fearful or cowardly who enter hell (Rev. 21:8). And so on.

But a man might say that fear is an emotion he

35

cannot always control. Suppose I am about to be killed, or worse still tortured, can I avoid fear? Even in such circumstances, says Jesus, it is still wrong to fear. 'I tell you my friends, do not fear those who kill the body, and after that have no more that they can do. But I will warn you whom to fear; fear him who, after he has killed, has power to cast into hell; yes I tell you fear him!' (Lk. 12:5).

It is this doctrine, the doctrine that if it comes to the choice we must dread God rather than people, which saves a man from the possibility of being brain-washed; for the technique of brain-washing depends upon playing upon a man's hopes and fears. If the prisoner utterly refuses to become involved, if he is much more concerned to please his heavenly Father than his tormentors, he cannot be brain-washed. For the same reason insane people cannot be brain-washed, because it is not possible to make them feel involved in their fate.

Violence and fear are close bed-fellows. A man will commit murder if he fears that if he does not strike the preemptive blow, his enemy will do so. People who are involved in a movement which resorts to violence fear that if they opt out they will be liquidated.

In national wars fateful decisions are often dictated by fear. In World War 1 the German high command, fearing that the war would drag on interminably in the absence of a quick decision, resorted to the use of poison gas. The story of how the atom bomb came to be invented and used in World War 2 has been told often enough: it was the fear, indeed the sheer dread (quite unwarranted as it turned out) that Hitler would make it first which led to Einstein's famous letter to Roosevelt and the subsequent all-out effort to make the bomb.

The appalling evils which can result from fear are well illustrated by the story of the witchcraft trials which for two centuries (roughly 1500–1700) were the scourge of Christendom.

Towards the close of the 15th century rumours spread abroad that the many natural calamities and misfortunes – storms, low yields of crops and vines, children born misshapen, epidemics, and so on – arose because certain evilly disposed persons were invoking the power of the devil to harm mankind. In 1484 Pope Innocent VIII in a famous Bull declared that the rumours were all too true and he appointed two Inquisitors, Kramer and Sprenger, to seek out, bring to judgment and punish those responsible. The faithful were called upon everywhere to aid them in their work.

Before long the witchcraft scare snowballed. Sheer terror was caused by rumours of what secret covens of witches had done or were planning to do next. It was said that witches abducted children and sacrificed them to the devil, ate human flesh, raised storms which wrecked ships, defiled the sacraments, enjoyed sexual orgies with devils, killed whom they willed by their spells and turned themselves into dogs and cats to avoid detection. They had the devil-given power to transport themselves unnoticed where they chose, hidden if need be in black clouds, and carried perhaps on broomsticks (instead of aeroplanes!).

There was no telling when or where witches would next perform their abominations: their actions were as unexpected and sudden as those of the bomb planters, hijackers or guerrillas of today.

Though witches were deemed rare before 1500, it was not long before their numbers were believed to have increased prodigiously. In Mary's reign the 'number of witches and sorcerers had everywhere become enormous' (Bishop Jewel, 1559); 'The land is full of witches, they abound in all places' (Lord Chief Justice Anderson, 1602). It was widely believed on the continent that a wizard named Treiseschelles, had openly boasted to King Charles IX of France that there were 300,000 (though some said he had mentioned only 30,000) witches within his domain and that all were ready, at an agreed signal, to depose him from his throne and take over the ship of state in the name of the devil. From every quarter, every hamlet even, tales circulated about the formation of more and yet more covens of witches.

The language of the old books is so quaint to our ears and some of the tales so silly to our way of thinking (like the one about the devil-possessed nun through whom the devil explained to an angry priest that while he, the innocent little devil, was quietly sitting on a lettuce leaf, the nun came and ate him up without warning, so of course the good lady was possessed!) that often we cannot restrain a smile. But in those days witchcraft was no laughing matter. Men and women believed what was said and were petrified with fear. In Geneva on 2 Dec. 1555 Calvin preached a sermon in which he said, 'If we hear of these matters, that is of the incredible things we learn about sorcerers, we must be seized by fear, the hairs of our heads must stand up on end.' (Quoted, O. R. Pfister, *Christianity and Fear*, 1948.)

In their dealings with witchcraft what were decent God-fearing men to do? A few, a very few, were openly sceptical. (This happened especially in England where the terror was much less intense than on the continent owing to Henry VIII's break with Rome and the fact that torture had long been illegal save for treason.) On the continent an expression of disbelief was usually taken as an insult to holy church and even as evidence of complicity in witchcraft, for which a man would be tortured, tried and burnt.

In view of the enormity of the sin of witchcraft most people thought that the only possible course was to dispense with human decency and Christian principles. The church was clear on this point: there was no need to keep faith with heretics. It is laid down in Kramer and Sprenger's famous *Hammer of the Witches* that a judge may promise to be merciful to a witch who confesses 'with the mental reservation that he means he will be merciful to himself or the State'.

At all costs it seemed necessary to rid society of a frightening menace. So men and women, chiefly women, poor, unprotected, innocent of high crimes against society, were starved, left to rot in sickly jails, tortured repeatedly till they confessed to imaginary crimes, then tortured again till they had incriminated others equally innocent and finally led to the stake to be strangled and then burnt, or burnt alive if at the last they again bravely declared their innocence. In many villages every human soul was found guilty and killed. Sometimes in the cruel cold winter when the burnings had made fuel scarce, some poor widow would bring her costly little offering of a faggot or two to help God in his glorious work of burning the witch.

What kind of men were they who did these things? A few (like the notorious Matthew Hopkins in England) sought monetary gain, but many were obviously sincere. 'They reason cogently according to their lights' says a historian, 'and not at producing maximal human sufferings but at the relief of mankind from a grievous plague' (W. Shumaker, *The Occult Sciences in the Renaissance*, 1972, p. 65). They believed that by inflicting pain they made it easier for witches to repent of their sins and receive God's forgiveness.

The books of the witch hunters show great learning: they quote their authorities in hundreds. They worked seemingly at great personal risk to themselves, becoming targets for the devil's arrows. Nor were the risks all imaginary: jails in those days harboured lice, rats, dirt and disease: a judge might easily become infected and this often happened. With no knowledge of modern medicine he would not unnaturally think he was himself bewitched: the devil and his henchmen were having their revenge.

Inquisitors were brave men.

Today we recoil with horror at the witchcraft story; we reflect that hundreds of thousands of innocent people were subjected in the name of Christianity and the welfare of the state to every conceivable torture and finally murdered. We remember that not only Roman Catholics but also many Protestants were implicated. If Innocent VIII started the witch hunt, it was Calvin in Geneva who, in 1545 attributed an outbreak of plague to the activities of sorcerers and witches in the village of Peney. With Calvin's full approval the women had their hands cut off and the men were pinched with red hot tongs – not in secret but publicly. All (34 in number) were killed, some being burnt to death. Even after the plague had ceased Calvin urged the more lenient Council of Geneva to find more cases to bring to trial. 'Thou shalt not suffer a witch to live' (Ex. 22:18 AV, but the witch of the Old Testament and the witch of Calvin's time had little in common) said the sacred book, and Calvin believed he should obey. Calvin was also responsible for the killing of Servetus, the Spanish doctor, on the ground of heresy (Pfister, pp. 412, 432).

Who can doubt that Calvin was a true Christian? He lived a pious life and the world owes him much. He is described as a warm-hearted loving man in his relationships with friends. He showed deep concern for the poor, urging pastors and deacons to seek out any who were in dire need and make provision for them. He was instrumental in the appointment of a physician and a surgeon for the poor. And yet . . .

And yet . . . The horror of what happened can

41

never be effaced. Why did it happen? Why did Christians, even if many of them were only nominal Christians, fail so signally to show the Christian spirit of love to their neighbours? It was because they were frightened, because they forgot that love casts out fear. We too can forget this. Fear of what an enemy might do can make us as cruel as the inquisitors of yesterday. More cruel, perhaps, for bombs and napalm are probably more terrible than the stake, and atom bombs can affect a generation not yet born.

3. *Thinking oneself superior – slavery*

The doctrine of the Fatherhood of God and the brotherhood of all mankind is rightly based on the Bible ('being then God's offspring', Acts 17:29) even though the Bible also insists that some men, by reasons of their sins, have turned themselves into children of the devil (Jn. 8:42f).

Despite the Fatherhood of God, there are many ways in which men are unequal; their endowments in respect of genes, ability, opportunity, wealth, privilege and so on differ greatly. But Christians hold that all are equally potential objects of God's love and forgiveness. If in one sense inequality arises because God at first chose to reveal himself to some people (Abraham, Moses and the prophets) rather than to others (the gentiles) it remains true 'that God shows no partiality, but in every nation any one who fears him and does what is right is acceptable to him' (Acts 10:35). We have no authority to belittle others, to treat them as inferior to ourselves, or as less than human. 'Whoever insults his brother shall be liable to the council, and whoever says, "You fool!" shall be liable to the hell of fire' (Mt. 5:22). 'In humility count others better than yourselves' (Phil. 2:3).

The precepts of Christianity have been and are disregarded by the bulk of mankind. History is largely the story of men despising and being despised. The rich and powerful despise the poor and weak – the clever, the ignorant – the Jew, the Samaritan – the upper caste, the lower – white people, the blacks (sometimes the other way round) – proud nationals and tribesmen, the common enemy or the alien.

So intense is this feeling that among many peoples lacking a Christian tradition it is usual to think of those outside their own group not as men but as animals. The tribesmen of New Guinea only used the word for 'man' for those of their own tribes: other men were considered as animals and hunted as such. In World War 2 the Japanese did not regard their enemies as men: when ordinary food was unobtainable Japanese soldiers were permitted to eat Americans but not their fellow Japanese for that would have been cannibalism. In World War 1 it was quite usual for Englishmen to refer to Germans as vermin or as subhuman. 'By his absolute disregard of all the rules for the conduct of civilized warfare he has repeatedly placed himself beyond the pale of civilized man and forfeited all right to consideration as a human being' (letter to the *Times*, 27

June, 1917), was a typical sentiment of the day – no doubt echoed also on the other side.

It is obvious that attitudes of this kind are contrary to the spirit of the New Testament. Yet here, as in the case of witchcraft, Christians have only too often fallen into the world's ways of thinking.

An instructive example of what we have been saying is afforded by slavery. Here the attitude underlying the custom is unmistakable. The slave is below you in dignity for he does not quite come up to the human standard. The Constitution of the United States prescribes a census every ten years but says that in the returns each slave shall be counted as only three fifths of a person. (The underlying theory behind apartheid in S. Africa today is the unspoken belief that the black races are of animal origin and not fully human as yet.) Therefore you have a right to use him as you would use a beast – provide for his needs (for we look after animals that are useful to us) but treat him as an inferior and expect him to work for you and to be obedient.

Christianity was born in a slave-owning society and outright condemnation of the practice would have been interpreted as rebellion against the state and so would have been counter-productive. Instead of condemning, Christians wisely undermined slavery from below. In the early churches slaves were not reckoned inferior to their masters and could be elected to positions of honour. In Paul's short letter to Philemon, carried back to his master by a runaway slave, Paul tells the master to treat the man as a 'brother beloved'. In the long run slavery could not survive in a Christian atmosphere. But before slavery could be abolished the legal system of the ancient Romans needed to be changed gradually by the nominally Christian emperors, so that the slave's lot became less harsh.

The African slave trade of modern times was started by the Portuguese in the 15th century, not without considerable theological misgivings. In later years much of it came into the hands of the British. In the past historians have tended to assume that the former vast wealth of Britain was largely due to profit made in the slave trade, but especially in the later years this was not so. Research has shown that the financial returns of the trade were, in fact, for the time quite modest. (Roger Anstey, *The Atlantic Slave Trade and British Abolition, 1760–1810*, 1975). Averaged over half a century the profit was 10% per annum in the British and less in the Dutch and French trades – vastly less, in fact, than profits made in the newly rising industries. Summarising his work Anstey says, 'we were led to the frightening awareness' that it was not high profit, but the fact that 'most of those involved in the slave trade saw their involvements as an "honourable" and even "genteel" pursuit' which kept the trade thriving.

The terrible story of which we read in history books came to a close, as far as the British Empire was concerned, in 1833 when, largely thanks to work by Quakers and the evangelical parliamentary party (Wilberforce and the Clapham sect, etc.) slavery was finally abolished.

It is one of the blots on the history of Christianity that Western Christian countries should have enriched themselves by the African slave trade. Slave keeping was condoned or even supported by bishops and by the missionary minded SPCK.

To this day enemies of Christianity often refer to slavery in support of their contention that, on the whole, Christianity has not benefitted mankind. They tend to forget, however, that slavery was the creation of avaricious traders rather than of Christians, and that abolitionists were usually actuated by Christian motives. They forget, also, that free thinkers gave little support to the anti-slavery campaign.

It is instructive to examine the arguments used by Christians who supported slavery: facsimilies of some of their writings have been reprinted in recent years by the Negro Universities Press of New York and the subject has been explored by a number of historians.

In one influential book called *The Christian Doctrine of Slavery* (1857, repr. 1969) the author (G. D. Armstrong), a Christian minister, argues that 'slave-owning does not appear in any catalogue of sins or disciplinable offences given in the New Testament'. Christians such as Philemon, he says, are not told to release their slaves or not to buy and sell them.

In a book of essays by several authors (*Letters: Pro-slavery Argument*, 1852, repr. 1968) the following arguments (several of them repeated by different authors) will be found.

Authorities (Drew, Harper etc.) are quoted in support of the view that slavery is 'the principal cause of civilisation' which must crumble in its absence. Slavery is 'deeply founded in the nature of man' and God has made it so: who are we to criticize?

The Old Testament told men to exercise dominion over beast and fowl and obviously other men were also included in this command for the Israelites were free to buy foreign slaves – 'they shall be your bondmen for ever'. The Law assumed slavery 'Thou shalt not covet thy neighbour's wife . . . nor his man-servant, nor his maid-servant' (i.e. his slaves).

Where there are no slaves, as in England, young children are set to work 12–18 hours a day in mines or mills and left to starve when old: slaves enjoy a happier life and are saved from having to compete for employment.

Slave owners are mentioned in the New Testament parables but always in a favourable light.

The beating and even branding of slaves is right and Christian because it teaches slaves a lesson and prevents the worse evils that would follow from rebellion.

Slavery is also backed by the authority of the State to which Christians must be subject.

Far from being a harmful institution, it was argued, the slave trade was highly beneficial. It removed the cannibal from his degrading surroundings and turned him 'into a nice happy slave – a

Sambo': it was 'a commerce of mercy, a missionary institution'. (Quoted, T. T. Takaki, *Pro-slavery Crusade*, 1971.)

At the political level the same applied. To be an abolitionist was utopian and foolish. Though Southern owners in the USA themselves objected to slavery, argued Basil Hall (about 1827) abolition is 'so completely beyond the reach of any human exertions' that even to discuss it is 'the most profitless of all possible subjects of discussion'. (Quoted, A. Y. Lloyd, *Slavery Controversy*, 1831–60, 1939, p. 23.) In England it was often urged that the prohibition of slavery would amount to economic suicide.

It will be immediately apparent how closely some of these arguments resemble those still used today by Christians who accept participation in violence. Sometimes the resemblance is quite startling – compare, for example, these passages:

Abolitionists 'sat upon chairs of Cuban mahogany, before desks of Brazilian rosewood, and used inkstands of slave-cut ebony; but "it would not do to go round and enquire into the pedigree of every chair and table". In a country like England total abstinence from slave produce was impossible, unless they wished to betake themselves to the woods and live on roots and berries'. (Quoted by Eric Williams in *Capitalism and Slavery*, 1944, p. 86.)

If the pacifist is not going to profit by war, 'it means entire separation from current civilisation.

48

It means a monastery in a prairie . . . it means abstinence from the food which is brought to his door by the aid of a navy'. Even scholarships at universities should be renounced since the money that was used in founding them came from war (P. T. Forsyth, *The Christian Ethic and War*, 1916, p. 46).

A well known instance of a Christian slave trader is that of the hymn writer John Newton (1725–1807) author of 'How sweet the Name of Jesus sounds' and other well known hymns.

In his early turbulent life Newton served in the Royal Navy, escaped, then worked for slave traders and, whilst returning to England in 1747 was converted in a storm at sea in which his ship nearly sank. Thereafter he continued slave trading and was appointed captain of a slave ship. At no time, he says, did scruples enter his mind. He held services for the slaves on board and believed that the slave trade afforded an excellent opportunity for reaching black men with the Gospel. The life of the captain of such a ship, he thought, was better than any other for 'promoting the life of God in the soul'. Often he fasted and prayed for his men. Twice he used the thumb screw to torture the slaves: on one occasion when a last desperate effort by the blacks to save themselves was crushed they sank into apathy which Newton interpreted as a change of heart produced by the God of peace.

In 1754 Newton came home for the last time. His voyage had been unusually successful – no slaves or crew had died. (The *average* death rate in the passage to America was 17%!) He was congratulated by all and gave thanks to God. He intended to sail again at the end of the year but in this he was prevented by illness. Only later did he realise how wicked he had been and then he did all in his power to help the abolitionists. 'Custom, example and interest had blinded my eyes. What I did, I did ignorantly, considering it as the line of life which Divine Providence had allotted me.'

3:
Does the Old Testament justify war?

WE NOW TURN to the biblical justification of war. We have seen how, in the past Christians have justified evils, such as the persecution of witches and the institution of slavery, by arguments based on the Old Testament. Today few if any Christians think these arguments are valid. But many take apparently similar arguments about war quite seriously. Are they right? It is time to examine what the Old Testament actually says on the subject.

In the Old Testament God's chosen people, the Israelites were sometimes commanded to fight their enemies, but only because their enemies, on account of their sins, had also become God's enemies ('. . . the land became defiled, so that I punished its iniquity, and the land vomited out its inhabitants . . . keep my charge never to practise any of these abominable customs which were practised before you, and never to defile yourselves by them . . .' Lev. 18:24–30).

The aggressive wars of the Old Testament are terrible enough in all truth but must be seen in this context. According to the Old Testament God did not allow them to take place at all until the sins of the heathen nations had reached a threshold (Gen. 15:16, 'The iniquity of the Amorites is not yet complete'). At the time of the conquest in Canaan sexual sins were rife (Lev. 18); children and young men, whose bones can be seen today, were burnt to propitiate the gods and it was quite often standard practice (so archaeologists tell us) to make a human sacrifice when the foundations of a new house were laid. At the time of the setting up of the monarchy the king of the Ammonites, not content with possessing the submissive men of Jabesh as slaves, declared, 'On this condition will I make a treaty with you, that I gouge out all your right eyes' (1 Sam. 11:2).

Before the invasion of Canaan the Israelites were told plainly that if they behaved in the ways of the nations they were fighting, they too would be destroyed ('. . . lest the land vomit you out, when you defile it, as it vomited out the nation that was before you', Lev. 18:28). The fact that they were Israelites, God's chosen people, would not save them.

It is the uniform teaching of the Old Testament that judgment must follow when wickedness in a society infects the entire population and men are so set in their ways that reform from within is unthinkable. The outstanding biblical example is, of course, Noah's Flood ('The wickedness of man was great in the earth and every imagination of the thoughts of his heart was only evil continually', Gen. 6:5). In this case judgment came by a God-sent natural calamity but the Old Testament repeatedly teaches that war can also be used by God as the agent of destruction. The armies of Israel were the means by which God wiped out the people of Canaan, but when God's chosen people rejected their God, foreigners were in their turn raised up for the purpose. (Eg. 'the king of Babylon, my servant', Jer. 25:9; 27:6; 'Assyria – rod of my anger', Is. 10:5.)

In reading the Old Testament in the 20th century it is natural to take it for granted that the chauvinism with which we are all too familiar provided the background of Israel's cultural heritage. In fighting other nations with religious zeal, is it not obvious, we ask, that they, like so many in our own day, were saying to themselves, 'My country right or wrong'? When we read the Old Testament more carefully, however, we soon realise that nothing can be further from the truth. For the Israelite one's own tribe or country could be wrong and often was: it then became the duty of the Israelite to fight his own kith and kin or to be 'disloyal' to his own side in time of war. In short the Old Testament teaches that loyalty to God is far more important than loyalty to one's country.

When Israel had sinned by worshipping Aaron's golden calf, the sons of Levi, who remained loyal to the Lord, were commanded, 'slay every man his brother' (Ex. 32:27). There was immediate talk of war when it was rumoured that the tribes across the Jordan were building an altar of their own in 'treachery . . . against the God of Israel' (Josh. 22:16) and war was only averted on the assurance that a memorial rather than an altar had been constructed. When the news spread that the men of Gibeah, of the tribe of Benjamin, had 'committed abomination and wantonness in Israel' and that the rest of their tribe would not take them to book, the 'men of Israel went out to battle against Benjamin' and as a result the tribe was nearly exterminated (Jud. 20). Jeremiah the prophet publicly told Zedekiah's men not to fight the invading army and was punished for his pacifism and apparent disloyalty. ('Let this man be put to death, for he is weakening the hands of the soldiers', Jer. 38:4.)

It is worth noting that there were rules of war in the Old Testament. Fighting on the Sabbath was forbidden and – of interest to the modern ecologist – the land was not to be made a waste. 'When you besiege a city for a long time, making war against it . . . you shall not destroy its (fruit) trees . . . you shall not cut them down. Are the trees of the field men that they should be besieged by you?' (Deut. 20:19).

These passages give little encouragement to the Christian who is prepared, willy nilly, to fight for king (or queen) and country in time of war, or in support of his fellow partisans in time of revolution. A Christian in a modern army who decides to take his cue from the Old Testament might refuse to fight on Sunday, or to destroy natural resources if ordered to do so. He would be right to turn his machine gun on his own officers if they blasphemed God or took his Holy Name in vain. Together with fellow Christian soldiers he should be prepared to march against cities in his own country where vice is widespread but goes unpunished. If he thinks his country is in the wrong, as he might well have thought at the time of the Suez crisis, it would be his duty to tell other soldiers not to fight. He might have to do the same if he was convinced that God had sent a foreign invader to punish his country for its sins.

Merely to defend participation in war or violence because God sometimes allowed (or commanded) it in the Old Testament, yet to forget the conditions and purposes of Old Testament war, is far from consistent. This is what slave holders did when they defended their practice because they found it in the Old Testament, but forgot, conveniently, that the Old Testament punishes with death the man who captures a man to sell him into slavery ('Whoever steals a man . . . shall be put to death', Ex. 21:16; Deut. 24:7). By this principle the captains and owners of ships bringing the human cargo to the new world should have been apprehended, tried and condemned to death.

However, let us face the issue. When we read the Old Testament today the aggressiveness, the cruelty and the exterminations create difficulties. Can we believe that God commanded them as the Bible says? Or is the Bible, as many suppose, quite unreliable when it claims to tell us what God said? The difficulty becomes much less formidable if we take the teaching of the Bible as a whole rather than isolating passages out of a wider context. It is reasonable to think that God teaches men in stages as they are able to bear it, and that because of the hardness of men's hearts God may sometimes tell them to do things which, though better than what they would otherwise have done, are far from being in accordance with the true will of God.

On a number of occasions the Old Testament makes it plain that this is the principle on which God works. When the elders of Israel demanded bluntly, 'Give us a king to govern us' (1 Sam. 8) God, speaking through Samuel, said, 'They have rejected me from being king over them'. Yet when they persisted, God told them to elect a king and showed them how to proceed. After Elijah had been taken up into heaven the prophets at Jericho urged Elisha to send out a search party. 'And he said, "You shall not send". But when they urged him . . . he said "Send".' Three days later the party returned empty-handed and Elisha 'said to them, "Did I not say to you, Do not go?"' (2 Kings 2:16–18). Balaam was told by God that he was not to visit Balak but when he persisted God told him to go but told him also what to say (Num. 22). Ezekiel is quite blunt in declaring that what God tells man to do is sometimes neither good nor right. Because Israel utterly rejected God's statutes, profaned God's sabbaths and worshipped idols, God said: 'I gave them statutes that were not good and ordinances by which they could not have life; and I defiled them through their very gifts in making them offer by fire all their first born that I might horrify them' (Ezek. 20:24f). Because the Israelites who had defied God's command not to go to Egypt went and there made vows that they would burn incense to the Queen of Heaven, Jeremiah, speak-

56

ing in the name of the Lord, said 'Go ahead then, do what you promised! Keep your vows!' (Jer. 44:25, NIV). Paul re-echoes much the same thought: 'God gave them up' to vile sins (Rom. 1:20); 'because they refused to love the truth . . . therefore God sends upon them a strong delusion, to make them believe what is false' (2 Thess. 2:10–11).

The point is plain. Defy God again and again and he may tell you to do something so wrong that you will be forced to stop and think. Ahab affords an example of this. He asked for God's guidance but had no intention of doing what God said. He demanded of the prophet Michaiah if he should fight against the men of Ramoth-Gilead. The answer came pat: 'Go up and triumph; for they will be given into your hand' (2 Chron. 18:14). Only after further probing did the prophet describe his vision of Israel as sheep that have no shepherd.

It is plain, then, that according to the Old Testament God's commands do not always or necessarily represent the will of God when they are given to rebellious and hard-hearted people. This is no surprise: a good earthly father will sometimes find it necessary to act in the same way. It may prove quite useless to keep on saying 'Don't!' to a child who persists in playing with fire: it will sometimes be wiser to tell him to do just what he wants to do so that he may learn, but under controlled conditions, what it feels like to be burnt. It is hardly to be expected that God will never act in this way.

We know from the entire Old Testament story that God's people, the Israelites, were perverse, unappreciative and disobedient: whole chapters of the Old Testament are devoted to stressing this point, especially in the Psalms (eg. Ps 106). Therefore we cannot look for isolated passages in the Old Testament in which wars were commanded and assume that these wars were good in themselves, or that the Old Testament can be used to justify participation in war today. On such a basis we could prove from Ezekiel's words that God approves of burning children in fire or from Jeremiah's that God approves of idolatry! We must probe more deeply if we are to get near the heart of God.

Before continuing, it is worth noting that the Law itself, the very Law which commanded war, is presented to us in the Bible very much as a 'second best', an alternative approach by God to man, necessary only because of man's wickedness. The Mosaic Law was originally given shortly after the murmuring Israelites were at the point of stoning Moses (Ex. chs. 17,19) and was later confirmed after they had worshipped the golden calf (Ex. chs. 32–34). In the *Epistle to the Galatians* (ch. 3) Paul argues cogently that the way to man's acceptance by God offered by the Law does not represent God's original intention. Long before the Law was given to Moses, it was revealed to Abraham that not works, but faith is what God requires. According to the Law life (Paul thinks here of eternal life) is a reward for good works, but from the beginning it was not so. The Christian gospel brings man back to the original truth. This is the argument Paul used to refute the teaching that Gentile Christians ought to be circumcised and keep the law of Moses. Here, as so often with Paul, the thinking, though not the phraseology, follows that of Jesus.

At this point we must ask whether in fact the Israelites became better people than they might otherwise have been as a result of the way God dealt with them. The Old Testament seems to show that they did, for a time at least. Solomon's reputation was proverbial in his day: he was a man of peace who thought seriously about moral issues as we may see in the book of Proverbs. In his reign there was progress in the art of building and craftsmanship was much respected (2 Chron. 2). Even as late as Ahab's time the kings of Israel had the reputation in foreign countries of showing mercy. (Benhadad's servants said to their master, 'Behold now, we have heard that the kings of the house of Israel are merciful kings'. 1 Kings 20:31.) Though the practice was widespread in ancient times, there is never a suggestion in the Old Testament that prisoners might be tortured – a fact which witch hunters, and slave traders and owners of later times conveniently overlooked. The historian Gibbon speaks of the all but universal custom for a king, on ascending a throne, to kill his brothers, lest they became claiments to the throne. This was condemned in Israel (Jud. 9:56). It is true that Solomon did kill his brother Adonijah, but Adonijah might have lived had not he planned rebellion (1 Kings 2:19f). In many other ways, too, the laws and practices of the Israelites were surprisingly humane and just. (The subject is

59

discussed in some detail in J. W. Wenham's *The Goodness of God*, 1974.)

These examples show that, despite the terrible nature of much in the Old Testament, the nation of Israel was raised morally above the level of surrounding nations. In later times this was widely recognized in the pagan world. By the time of Christ vast numbers of non-Jews worshipped in Jewish synagogues throughout the Roman world. (For a scholarly account of 'The Jewish Dispersion in New Testament Times' see I. H. Marshall, *Faith and Thought*, 1973, vol. 100(3), 237–258.)

In the New Testament it is very clear that Jesus interpreted the Old Testament in the light of the principle we have set out. When Jesus condemned divorce he was reminded that it had the sanction of Moses. In reply he refuses to admit that appeal to the Old Testament justifies divorce; on the other hand he does not say that Moses was wrong, or had made a mistake in interpreting God's law. Instead, he appeals to the principle that when people are bent on doing wrong it is often best to tell them to carry on with it, but to regulate, if possible, how they do it. 'For the hardness of your heart Moses allowed you to divorce your wives, but from the beginning it was not so' (Mt. 19:8).

At the end of his life Jesus himself acted as Moses had acted in ancient times. Judas was fully determined to go ahead with the betrayal. In tenderest love Jesus tried to win him back (he even washed his feet) but to no avail. Finally, at the last supper, he said to Judas bluntly, 'What you are going to do, do quickly' (Jn. 13:27). It was a command, a command to do something evil. Would this shake Judas, a command to betray him coming from the Lord himself? . . . It did not and Jesus was betrayed. But no one in their senses would dream of using these words, out of context, to justify a betrayal today.

Then how do we know God's will if we cannot always take his commands at their face value? There is but rarely any difficulty. The character of God, as given in the Old Testament, gives us a cue. 'The Lord, the Lord, a God merciful and gracious, slow to anger, and abounding in steadfast love and faithfulness, keeping steadfast love for thousands, forgiving iniquity and transgression and sin' (Ex. 34:6), though punishing those who persist in wrongdoing. The distorted commands come as a result of rebellion (Moses on divorce, Ahab, Balaam, Judas, Rev. 22:11 etc.); much more rarely, perhaps, to test faithfulness and loyalty (Abraham and Isaac, the command to the Recabites to drink wine, Jer. 35:2,5). The commands which tell us God's will come at the beginning, or they are implied, hinted at, or stated in many places in the Bible.

There is no need, then, to seize upon the darker passages of the Old Testament as expressions of Jehovah's heart. The Israelites, flushed with victory, expressed cruel sentiments at times – as in the blood-thirsty song which blesses Jael for murdering

Sisera (Judges 5:23) and in the imprecatory Psalms. These passages (which rarely if ever claim divine inspiration) express the sentiments of men rather than of God. The general tone of the Bible is very different.

As in the case of divorce there is much in the Old Testament to suggest that God is displeased with the use of violence by man. God put a mark upon Cain, the first murderer, lest anyone finding him should kill him (Gen. 3:15); the punishment imposed was banishment, not death. Capital punishment for murder was only commanded after the Flood, for without it the world had become filled with violence.

On several occasions foreign armies are dealt with without the need for shedding of blood by man. Pharoah's host did not need to be destroyed in pitched battle: 'The Lord will fight for you and you have only to be still' (Ex. 14:14). Benhadad's soldiers were sent back to their master after being given a good meal (2 Kings 6:15–24). The word of the Lord came to David saying, 'You have shed much blood and have waged great wars, you shall not build a house to my name, because you have shed so much blood before me upon the earth' (1 Chron. 22:8). God was pleased that Solomon did not ask for the life of his enemies (2 Chron. 1:11) and he was allowed to build the temple because he was a man of peace.

In later days God's hatred of war and killing shone through more clearly. 'Have I any pleasure in the death of the wicked, says the Lord God, and not rather than he should turn from his way and live . . . I have no pleasure in the death of anyone' (Ezek. 18:23, 32; repeated 33:11).

In such passages as these we can see the love of God. If in old time God had simply told his people not to fight or shed blood, what would have happened? They would simply have disobeyed. So he told them to fight – but to fight for righteousness, not for themselves but for their God. Even so, any who felt that fighting was wrong must often have found military service easy to avoid – a man who had recently married, or built a house, or planted a vineyard or merely felt nervous, was automatically excused military service (Deut. 20:5–8; 24:5).

The fact is that resort to violence as we know it today, in war or revolution, is not at the Jewish level at all, but at a sub-Jewish level: it cannot be defended by appeal to the Old Testament. Today war increasingly involves the killing of the innocent which is the very possibility which horrified Abraham. 'Far be it from thee to do such a thing, to slay the righteous with the wicked, so that the righteous fare as the wicked! Far be that from thee! Shall not the Judge of all the earth do right?' (Gen. 18:25).

4:
What does the New Testament say?

IF RESORT TO violence is always wrong for Christians, why does not the New Testament say so clearly? Why does not John the Baptist tell the soldiers who came to him for advice to leave their calling? Why did Jesus himself set an example by using force when he used a whip in the Temple? Why was it that on one occasion he told his disciples to buy swords? Why do the parables and similies of the Gospels freely draw upon the military career for analogies? Are these facts compatible with the view that fighting is unchristian?

So run the usual arguments. Before embarking on the main issue of the teaching of Jesus on violence, let us dispose of a few of the minor points first.

In John (2:14f) we read that on his visit to the temple Jesus 'found those who were selling oxen and sheep and pigeons and the money-changers at their business. And making a whip of cords he drove [them] all (*pantas*) out of the temple'. At first sight, in English, the 'all' refers to the people mentioned. But the word for 'them' is not present in the Greek and the 'all' clearly refers to what follows, 'both the sheep and the oxen', not to the *people* mentioned (lit. '. . . all he expelled out of the temple, both the sheep and the oxen').

That this is the meaning is also clear from the context. Whips would normally be used on cattle, not men. After Jesus had driven 'all' out, the *men* who sold doves were still there, for Jesus turned to them next telling them to remove their goods: 'Take these things hence'. The 'all' cannot therefore refer to men but to cattle.

The case of the swords (Lk. 22:36) is perhaps more difficult: many suggestions have been made. Some have supposed that literal swords were not intended for how could two swords defend a dozen men? Yet when he was told that the disciples had two, Jesus at once said that no more were needed! ('Look, Lord, here are two swords. And he said to them, It is enough'.)

However, the meaning seems to be provided by the context. 'For I tell you that this scripture must be fulfilled in me, "And he was reckoned with transgressors"; for what is written about me has its fulfilment' (v. 37). Jesus wanted his disciples to fulfil the prophecy. To an outsider it must appear plausible that Jesus and his disciples were a band of robbers. So he asked them to provide purses and bags, for robbers would not live on charity! And the presence of a weapon or two would help to make the robber theory plausible to the outsider – two would be plenty, perhaps more than enough. (NEB 'Enough! Enough! he replied'.)

We may see here a beautiful instance of the way in which God, in his love, seeks to reduce man's guilt. Some of those who arrested Jesus, among them servants of the High Priest, probably knew nothing of the evil motives of those in high authority. They were simply obeying orders. The sight of purses, bags and swords would have set their minds at rest: they were doing the right thing in arresting a robber band. Even if this interpretation is wrong, the fact which stands out plainly is that when Peter started to use one of the swords, he was at once not only rebuked (Mt. 26:52; Lk. 22:51) but Jesus took the opportunity to teach the disciples the principle that 'they that take the swords shall perish with the sword'. It is even possible that Jesus wanted one or two of his disciples to be armed in order to teach them this lesson in a practical way. In the one episode in history in which, more than in any other, force seemed called for, Jesus says that the sword is forbidden.

However we may choose to explain these two examples, they are certainly most exceptional in the Gospels – a fact which no one questions. It cannot be right, therefore, to cite them as a norm on which we may base our own conduct.

However, in mentioning these two apparent justifications of force in the New Testament Christians sometimes forget that there is force *and* force. Punishment can sometimes be administered in a manner compatible with the Golden Rule of doing unto others what we should like them to do to us. As a boy at school the writer was once soundly thrashed for being lazy at his lessons. Though it seemed unfair for a day or so, he soon learned to be grateful for the punishment. Obviously, force, even violence, can be rightly used on rare occasions especially in the disciplining of children. Perhaps some of those whose animals were thrown out of the temple later felt grateful for this reminder that they had no business to be trading there. All would have realised, if they were honest, that God took priority over their profit making. When men speak of force, or of violence, today, they mean something quite different. They mean killing and maiming, attacking innocent people in their homes or at their work. No one is grateful to the man who shoots at him with a gun, who maims him for life with a bomb, who kills his wife and children. Nor does anyone suppose that Jesus used this kind of force on men. The Apostles James and John thought of doing so on one occasion ('Do you want us to bid fire come down from heaven and consume them?' Lk. 9:54) but Jesus 'turned and rebuked them'.

What of some of the other arguments? Why did neither John the Baptist nor Jesus tell soldiers to leave their calling?

At the debating level it might be retorted that Jesus did not specifically forbid his disciples to persecute witches, to own, buy or sell slaves, to be cruel to animals, to take drugs, or to overcharge for goods and services. It is more relevant, perhaps, to point out that as Jews were not conscripted into the Roman armies, the question of conscientious objection as such did not arise for them. We shall return to the subject in the sequel.

What of the argument based on parables? It is evident that people mentioned in the New Testament parables and analogies are chosen to illustrate certain qualities, regardless of whether the profession or calling in question is right or wrong. Thieves in particular act suddenly and unexpectedly but when the New Testament compares God to a thief (Mt. 24:43; Rev. 3:3 etc.) it is not to commend the thief's way of life. The same point applies to the parable of the unjust judge (Lk. 18:6), while in another parable a dishonest steward is commended (Lk. 16:9). These parables are not intended to justify judges when they act unjustly, or stewards when they defraud their employers – and no one would think of so using them. The analogies are apt in their context – the dishonest steward, for example, because he was so astute. Similarly the qualities of alertness, loyalty and self-discipline found in soldiers have their counterpart in the life of a Christian: he too can be a soldier of Jesus Christ (Phil. 2:25; Cf. the hymn 'Onward Christian soldiers'). The same applies to sport. Paul draws analogies from both running and boxing. Again, there are no overtones of approval or disapproval of these activities implied. Stealing, falsifying an employer's books, fighting, running, boxing: all provides illustrations. But drunkeness and adultery do not, not because they are wrong (which they certainly are), but because they do not call forth qualities which we can all emulate.

Another argument sometimes heard is that Christians should 'be subject to the governing authorities' (Rom. 13:1. See also 1 Pet. 2:13–14;

Titus 3:1). If therefore authorities introduce conscription in time of war, Christians should obey. (See Appendix on Rom. 13.)

However, it is certain that the apostles did not intend their words to be used in this way. Paul tells children to obey their parents and servants their masters. But suppose a parent tells his child to steal, or a master tells his servant to commit murder. Ought they to obey? Did Daniel do wrong in disobeying Nebuchednezzar, or Joab right in obeying king David in the matter of Uriah the Hittite? Of course not.

The Christian should be a loyal citizen; not a violent revolutionary: that is the teaching of Scripture. He should seek the welfare of the State which, under God, ensures the safety of its citizens and punishes evil doers. But if a clash arises and the State tells the Christian to do what he knows to be wrong, it is clearly his duty to disobey. To hold any other view is to place the State above God. The apostles made this plain for all time when, after they had been sternly charged by the authorities of the day not to teach in the name of Jesus, they replied: 'Whether it is right in the sight of God to listen to you rather than to God, you must judge' (Acts 4:19).

All down history there have been times when the demands of the State and the commands of God have clashed. The State demanded of early Christians that they should offer incense to the genius of the Emperor, but the Christian of those days often preferred martyrdom. At various times and places down history it has been illegal to possess a copy of the Bible, to attend a place of worship or to aid a man fleeing for his life. Christians in the past have often, and rightly, disobeyed the State when it made such demands. And not Christians only, but Jews. The Jewish Talmud lays it down that 'If the law of the state is in conflict with religious and moral laws, one must disobey the state.'

To obey the State in all circumstances would be contrary not only to Christian pacifism but also to the doctrine of the just war. It would mean that a man might have to fight on the side he knew to be in the wrong. No Christian could agree to this.

We now come to the important question. Why did not Jesus teach plainly that joining armies and fighting are wrong, if wrong they are?

Is the premise right? The words spoken to Peter when he tried to prevent his Master's arrest might lead one to doubt it. 'Put your sword back into its place; for all that take the sword will perish by the sword' (Mt. 26:52). Again, in the Sermon on the Mount (Mt. 5) Jesus says 'Blessed are the peacemakers for they shall be called sons of God'. He extends the law 'You shall not kill' so that it covers even anger, or insulting behaviour, or saying 'You fool!' (meaning worthless fellow). Is it conceivable that he did not extend it to doing the things which armed men do to one another? He says also, 'Do not resist one who is evil. But if any one strikes you on the right cheek, turn to him the other also'.

Do these sayings apply to war – civil or national?

Many suppose that they do not. Often it is argued (with Luther) that only personal enemies are in question. But can this interpretation be defended? A careful reading of the passage in its context should give us the answer.

The part of the Sermon on the Mount which comes closest to the question of fighting in war is this:

> You have heard that it was said, You shall love your neighbour and hate your enemy. But I say to you, love your enemies and pray for those who persecute you, so that you may be sons of your father who is in heaven; for he makes his sun to rise on the evil and on the good, and sends rain on the just and on the unjust. For if you love those who love you, what reward have you? . . . You therefore must be perfect as your heavenly Father is perfect (Mt. 5:43–48).

What does this mean? All Christians agree that personal enemies are intended, but are enemies of other kinds intended also? The passage certainly suggests this.

Paraphrasing the argument in the language of today, we might say that since God has so made the world that the good gifts of sunshine and rain are bestowed upon all men, whether good or evil, we too must copy God by showing kindness to the evil as well as to the good. This would seem to imply that Christians must be kind to tribal, national or political enemies as well as to private ones, for they receive sunshine and rain just as we do.

However, the point is easily settled. We note that

all through the passage our Lord has been contrasting his own teaching with what 'was said'. On each of the previous occasions he started with an accurate quotation from the Old Testament (v. 27 'You shall not commit adultery'; v. 31, 'Whoever divorces his wife, let him give her a certificate of divorce'; v. 33, 'You shall not swear falsely, but shall perform to the Lord what you have sworn'; v. 38, 'An eye for an eye and a tooth for a tooth'). He then proceeded to give his own teaching which was in contrast to that given to 'the men of old'. He did this as one speaking with authority, not as the scribes (Mt. 7:29).

Most emphatically this does not mean that Jesus repudiated the law: in this very chapter he says plainly that he did not come to destroy the law but to fulfil it (v. 17–20).

The very fact that there was a law about divorce at all implied an underlying principle in the law of faithfulness in marriage to which an exception was made. Jesus is not altering the law itself – the basic principle – but only the exception to it that was permitted. Similarly the law 'an eye for an eye and a tooth for a tooth' implied an underlying fundamental principle of justice. This rule was made so that men would not demand *more* than a just recompense, a point well understood by the Pharisees. It was a statute of limitation: underlying it was the hope that a man would not demand full recompense, or even any recompense at all. It is this underlying principle which Jesus brings into the open. No wonder He could say, 'Think not that I am come to abolish the law and the prophets; I have come not to

72

abolish them but to fulfil them' (v. 17).

What then about the exceptions allowed by the Old Testament? We have already seen that Jesus endorsed the Old Testament teaching that because of the hardness of mens' hearts God had sometimes told his people in past ages to act in ways which were not in harmony with the basic principles of his will. But in the Sermon on the Mount Jesus urges men to return to the basic principles. Thus Moses told men that they could, under certain conditions, put away their wives but 'from the beginning it was not so'. Similarly the Old Testament allowed oaths, but Jesus said, 'Swear not at all'. A man who takes an oath to do something invites God's judgment if he fails to do what he promises, for that is what swearing means, even if it is euphemistically disguised (Mt. 5:34–6). But the follower of Jesus will say, 'I have sinned: I plead with God to forgive me, not to judge me.' Apart from this, to take an oath to speak the truth is to say in effect, 'Sometimes I tell lies, but on this occasion I will tell the truth', whereas a Christian must always be a man of his word.

In all instances there is a contrast between the old teaching and the 'But I say unto you' of Jesus. The contrast may take the form of forbidding what the law allowed, but always the original law or the principle which underlies it is made to apply much more widely than formerly. Thus adultery and murder are made to cover impure desire and hatred respectively.

In the first five instances, then, (killing, adultery, divorce, oaths, eye for eye) all is plain: the Old

Testament said one thing; Jesus by way of amplification contrasts his own teaching with what was taught before. He argues that the law, far from being set aside, must now be fully applied as was intended by God from the first.

But in the sixth and last contrast we meet a difficulty. According to Jesus the Old Testament teaching was 'You shall love your neighbour and hate your enemy'. Now the Old Testament certainly says, 'Love your neighbour' but the exact words 'Hate your enemy' are nowhere to be found. Nevertheless, Jesus clearly implies that the people of his day had been taught to hate their enemy and the context as clearly implies that Moses was responsible for this teaching.

The orthodox Christian view is that Jesus is referring to personal enemies, and because 'hate your enemy' is not to be found in the Old Testament we are to conclude that the Rabbis twisted the Old Testament to make it say just this. Such an allegation, direct or implied, is to be found repeated over and over again in scores of Christian books, old and recent. To quote from one of the latter (taken almost at random), '. . . and hate your enemy is nowhere to be found in the Old Testament . . . Matthew means by it the exegetical understanding of the Rabbis which they put into the mouth of the text'.

This is simply not true. Moses did not teach the Israelites to hate their private enemies. Nor did the Rabbis. Statements of this kind, especially when they are made by Christians of standing, inevitably have the effect of turning Jews against Christianity.

We may let Jews speak on this:

C. C. Montifiore rightly observes that we cannot
think very highly of the morality of that New
Testament author (St. Matthew) in inventing a
sentence unknown to the Torah in order to
depreciate the Torah. Canon Rawlinson admits
that 'hate thine enemy' was no injunction of the
Mosaic Law but maintains that it is a conclusion
which rabbinical teachers unwarrantably drew
from it. This charge against the Rabbis is utterly
false. It is Christian teachers who rarely
preached, and still more rarely practised, love of
those whom they branded as enemies . . . The
greatest hero, say the Rabbis, is he who turns an
enemy into a friend; and this can only be done by
deeds of loving kindness. (J. H. Hertz, ed., *The
Pentateuch and the Haftorahs*, 1930, p. 266.)

Many sayings in the Talmud and Midrash prove
that Jews were bound to love their enemies and to
forgive private wrongs. If a man found an enemy
and a friend both needing help, he was to help his
enemy first. 'Rejoice not when thine enemy fal-
leth and let not thine heart be glad when he
stumbleth' (*Aboth* IV, Etc. *Jewish Encyclopaedia*, Art. Enemy).

There is no doubt at all that the Jews are right.
Every Christian who has read the Old Testament
knows full well that it contains not the slightest
suggestion that a private enemy may be hated. On
the contrary it is taught emphatically that he must

be loved – at least in the practical sense that he must be helped when in trouble:

'You shall not hate your brother in your heart, but you shall reason with your neighbour . . . you shall love your neighbour as yourself.' (Lev. 19:17). 'If your enemy's ox or his ass go astray, you shall bring it back to him. If you see the ass of one who hates you lying under his burden, you shall refrain from leaving him with it, you shall help him to lift it up'. (Ex. 23:4, 5). 'Do not say, 'I will repay evil', wait for the Lord and he will help you.' (Prov. 20:22). 'Do not rejoice when your enemy falls, and let not your heart be glad when he stumbles . . . Do not say "I will do to him as he has done to me"; I will repay the man back for what he has done.' (Prov. 24:17, 29). 'If your enemy is hungry, give him bread to eat; and if he is thirsty give him water to drink: for you will heap coals of fire on his head and the Lord will reward you.' (Prov. 25:21–22). Similarly in the Apocrypha – 'Forgive your neighbour the hurt that he hath done' (Ecclus. 28:2).

In accordance with this teaching, we find Job declaring that at no time did he sin by rejoicing 'at the ruin of him that hated me . . . I have not let my mouth sin by asking for his life with a curse' (Jb. 31:29). Again, Jeremiah, fearing that his prayer for the destruction of those who challenged God to do his worst ('Where is the word of the Lord? Let it come!') might seem to imply hatred on his part, says to God, 'I have not pres-

76

sed thee to send evil, nor have I desired the day of disaster, thou knowest' (Jer. 17:15–16).

In the light of these passages and of the teachings of the Rabbis, it is hardly surprising that the common explanation of our Lord's words proves offensive to Jews. If we accept it, all force in the contrast between the old-time teaching and the 'But I say unto you' of Jesus is lost, for the usual explanation makes our Lord say precisely what the Old Testament and the Rabbis said.

What then does the passage mean? There is no difficulty about the answer. How would a man have been understood who spoke of the 'enemy' in occupied Europe during World War 2? Of course Jesus meant the national enemy. In his own day that enemy was Rome which occupied his country. But the argument he uses shows clearly that he had in mind not Rome only but all tribal, political and national enemies down all history. God is kind, even to our political opponents and the foreign invader: you must be kind too.

'You shall love your neighbour and hate your enemy.' Now 'neighbour' in the Old Testament means, not a private friend, but a fellow God-fearing Israelite (see Lev. 19:17f). And although the precise words 'hate your enemy' do not occur in the Old Testament, they are a fair summary of the law in so far as an enemy of the nation is concerned:

Nations which had been cruel to Israel were to be hated. Of Ammon and Moab it is said: 'You shall not seek their peace or their prosperity all your days for ever' (Deut. 23:6). 'Remember what

Amalek did to you on the way as you came out of Egypt . . . therefore when the Lord your God has given you rest from all your enemies round about . . . you shall blot out the remembrance of Amalek from under heaven; you shall not forget' (Deut. 25:17f). A number of the Psalms contain expressions of national hatred, for example, 'Do I not hate them that hate thee, O Lord . . . I hate them with perfect hatred: I count them mine enemies' (139:21–22); 'O daughter of Babylon, you devastator! . . . Happy shall he be who takes your little ones and dashes them against the rock!' (137:8). Jews still have no objection to such hatred: 'Where there are indications in the Bible of a spirit of hatred and vengeance toward the enemy, they are for the most part purely nationalistic expressions, hatred of the national enemy being quite compatible with an otherwise kindly spirit' (*Jewish Encyclopaedia*, Art., Enemy).

No Jew could have misunderstood what Jesus said. They thought it right to hate the Romans: to hate any national enemy. They had every cause to hate. Thousands of Jews had been cruelly done to death by the Romans. As a boy Jesus could hardly have scrambled around the countryside without coming across the graves of some of the several thousand Jews who had been killed near Nazareth shortly before his parents settled there. The Old Testament said 'Hate!' but Jesus said 'love your enemy'. Could he have expressed himself more clearly?

'Love your enemies'. That is just what Jesus did. He risked his reputation by making friends with tax gatherers – the fifth columnists who were making money out of being friendly with the enemy. He gave no encouragement to Zealots or other groups which aimed at insurrection against Rome. When foreign soldiers came and demanded service, he told the people not merely to do what was demanded but to do more, to go the second mile. Christ's motives were not political – he acted as he did out of love and because hatred of the national enemy is wrong. It makes you unlike God who is good to all men. But if you want to be his sons, then you must be like him, you must be perfect as he is perfect, you must imitate him in his dealings with men. If you love your countrymen only what do you more than others?

We Christians can hardly avoid the conclusion that what applied to the Roman enemy applies to all enemies all down the world's history. It is still true today that God is kind to the unthankful and evil as well as to the good. Our duty then is the same now as it was then.

'Love your enemies'. How is it possible when women are raped, property destroyed, loved ones murdered or taken away? We can only say that many of Christ's commands are given in the full knowledge that we cannot in ourselves obey them. Can we in ourselves do even the first and most elementary of His commands – to love the Lord our God with all our minds, our souls, our strength? It is this fact which has so often led men to find their salvation in Christ. Only when we come to God recognizing our utter inability to please him in our own strength is he able to receive us. And then he is able to give us the strength to do what would otherwise be impossible – even to love those whom otherwise we should loathe and detest.

But having said this, we should remember also that the word 'love' has more than one meaning. Our Lord is using it here in the sense in which Moses used it: 'love your neighbour'. This did not mean that there was to be a sentiment of love between every man and his fellow-Israelite. It referred rather to practical kindness and consideration. (See Ex. 23:4–5 quoted above.) 'Love your enemies', then, bears the same meaning.

It means that, even if he is not personally endeared to you, you are not to seek his harm and you must help him in distress. 'You shall love your neighbour as yourself'. It is in this practical sense that we love ourselves, feeding ourselves when we are hungry, shielding our bodies from danger, but not necessarily liking our own personalities! And it is in this practical sense also that we are to love our enemy. We must not do to the enemy in times of war, civil strife or political upheaval anything which we should refuse to do to our own countrymen, faction or party.

If the soldiers of a foreign army demand that we should go with them one mile, we must show our practical love for them by going two (Mt. 5:41). If people persecute us, we must pray for them (v. 44). We must not boycott the enemy for our Lord adds in the very passage that we have been considering: 'For if you love them who love you, what reward have you? Do not even the tax gatherers do the same? And if you salute only your brethren (fellow Jews, nationals or party members) what are you doing more than others? Do not even the Gentiles do the same?' (v. 46–7). The rest of the New Testament also bears witness to this teaching:

> Repay no one for evil . . . if possible . . . live peaceably with all. Beloved, never avenge yourselves, but leave it to the wrath of God; for it is written, Vengeance is mine, I will repay says the Lord. No. 'If your enemy is hungry feed him, if he is thirsty give him drink; for by so doing you will heap burning coals upon his head'. Do not be overcome by evil, but overcome evil with good (Rom. 12:17–21).

From this teaching of our Lord and of the rest of the New Testament, which teaches over and over again that we are to love one another (including quite obviously, fellow Christians in a country at war with our own, or those in some other and hated group), to harm no one, to be kind and considerate, wise as serpents but harmless as doves, and so forth, one conclusion seems forced upon us. Participation in war, national, or civil, and preparation for it, is, for the Christian, sinful. It violates the most important command Christ ever gave – the command to love. It puts loyalty to the State or to a party above loyalty to Christ and friendship with one's fellow countrymen or party members, whether Christian or not, above friendship with fellow disciples.

We started by asking why, if it is wrong for a Christian to participate in war, the New Testament and especially Jesus himself did not say so clearly. The answer is that it is difficult to imagine how this teaching *could* have been expressed more clearly. It is, as we have seen, impossible to exclude the national enemy in the words 'Love your enemies'.

5:
Christians and war – the story

IF THE ARGUMENT we have developed is correct, Jesus told his followers not to join sides in the violent disputes of this world. They were to be peace makers, not partisans, in conflicts.

However, if this is what Jesus actually taught, we might expect his early disciples also to have understood him in this sense. After all, it was easier for them to interpret his teaching than it is for us. What, then, did they understand him to say about participation in violence? Did they refuse military service?

It is a historical fact that for two centuries Roman soldiers who became Christians refused any longer to carry arms and, in many instances, were martyred for their refusal. The fact that some of these martyrs (eg. Maximilian, martyred in 295 AD) were canonized by the church in later times shows that they were not isolated eccentrics. Speaking of the writings of the Christian fathers in this period, R. H. Bainton writes: 'All the outstanding writers of the East and West repudiated participation in warfare for Christians'. (*Harvard Theological Review*, 1946, *39*, 189. See also his book *Christian*

Attitudes towards War and Peace, 1961. Also C. J. Cadoux, *The Early Church and the World*, 1940 and Jean-M. Hornus, *'It is not Lawful for me to Fight'*, 1981.)

The early Christian attitude is the more striking in view of the fact that in those days there was but one civilized government in the world – the Roman, which had endured for a thousand years. Its soldiers were, in a sense, the policemen of the world. The only wars that Rome knew were frontier wars against savages (barbarians) and occasionally against rebels. In the first written criticism of the Christian faith of which we have knowledge, Celsus (about 170–180 AD) argues that the pacifism of Christians will be the world's undoing if Christianity prospers. 'If all men were to do the same as you' he writes, 'there would be nothing to prevent the king from being left in utter solitude and desertion and the forces of the empire would fall into the hands of the wildest and most lawless barbarians.' From this passage it seems that Celsus, writing in Rome, had never heard of a Christian who was not a pacifist.

From the end of the second century some Christians served in the army and, in the Eastern frontier of the empire, a few were engaged in battle. Nevertheless it appears to have been most exceptional at this period for a Christian to fight.

In discussing the early relationships of Christianity to war we must bear in mind that the duties of a soldier in those days covered much which, today, would be done by the police, Post Office, Fire Service and Civil Service. The army transported mails, looked after prisoners and, in Rome, organized the fire service. From the second century to the time of Constantine Christians were usually taught that, if they had been converted when in the army, they should remain at their work in peace time but that they should refuse to receive training in killing and should leave the army at once if called upon to fight. (These injunctions were laid down, for example, at the Council of Arles, 314 AD.) 'Ecclesiastical authors before Constantine condemned Christian participation in warfare but not necessarily military service in time of peace.' (Bainton). As late as the fourth century it is known that very many who became Christians left the army and when, in the time of Constantine, the nominal church at last began to come to terms with war, a vast number of Christian, still resolutely rejecting military service, became ascetics.

In later times the Church interpreted the refusal of the early Christians to bear arms to mean, only, that in pre-Constantine days a soldier's life was one in which idolatry could not be avoided. This explanation is still given in some Roman Catholic and Protestant circles, but it is quite inadequate. Christians would not have remained in the army in peace time if army life necessarily involved idolatry. The evidence that what early Christians objected to in army service was not incidental temptations but killing itself is strong. 'Christ, in disarming Peter, ungirt every soldier' writes Tertullian. 'I threw down my arms: for it was not seemly that a Christian man, who renders service to the Lord Jesus Christ, should render it also by inflicting earthly injuries' said Marcellus, an early martyr, to his judge before his martyrdom.

When, in the time of Constantine, Christianity was officially adopted as a state religion, a compromise was sought. Had the church maintained its pacifism, it could never have won recognition. After Constantine's death (337 AD) Augustine of Hippo (354–430 AD) developed the theory of the just war – an idea which he borrowed from the pagan writer Cicero. This is still the official doctrine of the church, accepted by Roman Catholics, Lutherans and Anglicans. In its Latin form Article 37 of the Church of England states that Christian men may fight in 'just wars'.

In the middle ages the question was somewhat complicated by the resuscitation of a third view of war – that of the crusade. This way of thinking, taken over from the Old Testament invasion of Canaan, was used to justify the Crusades against the Turks. The enemy was now the epitomy of evil and deserved no consideration. In later years, as we have seen, the same attitude appeared in the war against witchcraft.

Returning to the just war (see F. H. Russell's, *The Just War in the Middle Ages*, 1975.) Augustine insisted that it must have the establishment of peace and justice as its aim. It must be waged only under the authority of the ruler and must be conducted in full awareness that enemies also are human beings. Looting, massacres, rape and destruction of places of worship are forbidden and no clergy, clerical or lay, may participate. The just war is to be prosecuted only to the point at which equitable retribution for wrong done has been effected: there must be no demand for unconditional surrender. From Augustine's time onwards it was realised that to punish an enemy beyond the point at which there had been fair retribution was bound to bring a desire for revenge. Men with their backs to the wall might well commit atrocities. 'That due terms and conditions are requisite to be offered ere war be undertaken . . . humanity itself teacheth; without which men would run upon one another with no less fury and disorder than beasts' (Bishop Hall, 1574–1656).

Again all Christians held that a war was only to be started as a last resort after every possible avenue of peace had first been explored. Once started it was to be conducted with no more fury or use of force than was strictly necessary. A war was not justified if, in prosecuting it, it was necessary to kill civilians who were not participants.

In World War 1 and more especially in World War 2 many Christians were troubled by an uneasy conscience. The difficulties in which the Anglican church felt itself placed were well set out in the document 'The Church and the Atom', 1948. In this a group of prominent Anglicans appointed by the Church Assembly and the Archbishops, discussed World War 2 in relation to the church's doctrine of the just war.

In certain respects the war was unanimously condemned. 'When the workers are in their factories, they have no more right than the personnel of a battleship to expect immunity from attack; but it is wrong deliberately to attack them in their homes' (p. 42). The Commission is agreed that the obliteration bombing of whole cities with high-capacity and incendiary bombs, the success of which is measured by the number of acres devastated, must be condemned. It is inconsistent with the limited end of a just war . . . it constitutes an act of wholesale destruction that cannot be justified' (p. 43).

A majority of the Commission thought that the use of atom bombs on Japan was wrong and all agreed that the supposed need to use them might never have arisen if the Allies had 'kept the law of the determinate end of war' in mind (p. 48–9). All agreed that the demand for unconditional surrender was wrong. Logic drove them to the conclusion that, though a Christian man might have joined the Forces in all sincerity in 1939, he ought to have refused to serve any longer either when 'obliteration bombing' started, or when the demand for unconditional surrender was made. But '. . . obviously we cannot deal adequately in this Report with so large and difficult a question'.

We are now beginning to see that events in modern times are making nonsense of the old Christian arguments for using force, whether against heretics or an enemy in time of strife. A condition laid down by all Christians in the past was that if you are constrained to use violence, you must use it as a surgeon uses his knife; in fighting your enemy you must seek his eventual good. It is always wrong to fight out of revenge or hatred.

History has dispelled this rationalisation. The Inquisition shows the murky depths to which this approach leads. In the auto-da-fè the witch is burnt at the stake, not because he is hated but because he is loved and his eventual salvation is desired. The pain you inflict will, it is hoped, help him to repent. But over the years the methods used – torture and fire in place of the sword – have brought only discredit, deep and terrible, to the Christian faith.

The doctrine of the just war laid it down as a condition that before resorting to war a Christian state must explore every possible avenue to a peaceful solution of differences: war can only be justified after all other methods have proved unavailing. Yet today no one doubts that this is exactly what was done in the case of Nazi Germany and it failed. If a pre-emptive war had been declared early in Hitler's career, the Nazi regime could never have become established.

In the past all wars were deemed wrong if it was necessary, in prosecuting them, to inflict suffering upon the innocent as well as upon the guilty. Today it is hardly possible to envisage a war in which women and children are not involved.

In the thirties many Christians turned to non-violent political action, seeing in Gandhi their paragon. If Gandhi could free his country from the British, might not his methods also be used effectively throughout the world? Few now believe this. It is commonly realised that Gandhi was successful only because he had the British to deal with. In another country he would have been locked up and the world would have heard no more of him.

A common argument is that fighting is sometimes the lesser of two evils – the evil of letting aggressors prosper and the evil of using violence against them. Even this argument is now much less plausible than in former times. No one can tell in advance what fighting may lead to. It may lead to a whole new generation brought up to hate and today's sophistication of weapons vastly increases the dangers. In a national war one side, rather than risk defeat, may deploy atomic weapons with devastating consequences for the whole world. Guerrilla warfare is safer yet far from safe: blackmail using stolen fissile material may well be the next headache mankind will have to face.

The idea of a just war held by generations of Christians is now a non-starter. Nor is any other compromise in view. How can the Christian raise his face today? Can he no longer speak with conviction: 'That is right: that is wrong!'?

What then can be done? All the compromises of Christians with the wickedness of men have proved an utter failure. At best the doctrine of the just war was like the Old Testament law about divorce – a compromise this time made by the church, but a compromise made none the less because of the hardness of mens' hearts. But is not this just the kind of compromise that Jesus condemned? Is it not time to take his teaching seriously again?

6:
What of the fight for justice?

UNTIL FIFTY YEARS AGO discussions on violence chiefly centred around national wars. If other nations behaved wickedly, was it right to declare war? Was war the lesser of two evils? Was it right for Christians to support their governments? Or could it be right to let evil triumph?

Today the focus of discussion has changed. The same distrust of other nations remains; it might easily be fanned into flame but politicians the world over are coming to realise that war is now a much less safe way of ensuring the triumph of justice than ever it was in the past. Weapons are now so shattering in their impact that the victorious side, like the defeated, might find recovery difficult – or even impossible. In World War 2 the Allies were well stocked with spores of anthrax: had the go-ahead to attack Berlin with this biological weapon been given, Berlin would have been made as uninhabitable to this day as is the Island of Gruinard where the trials were carried out. The use of atom bombs might prove more terrible and long lasting still. There is the added difficulty that after beating the foe a victorious army cannot easily advance into a defeated country if chemical, biological or nuclear weapons have been used.

Except in the case of small nations which at the present time are unable or unlikely to resort to the high technology of modern war, it is now realised that all-out war is unlikely to prove effective.

There is, of course, the ever present danger that war will be started by accident or perhaps by a madman in high office but, by and large, it is no longer safe to insist too vociferously on the sins of other nations lest demand for a just war should drive men over the edge of a precipice. Yet the desire to conquer and subjugate is far from dead. The methods used have changed to insurgency and revolution, but the result is the same. Other people are seen as wicked. In the past Christians had to decide whether to help a government fight people on the other side of a national frontier because the enemy had behaved so wrongly. Today they are often faced with whether to help revolutionaries in their efforts to destroy corrupt governments and so establish justice, or whether to refrain after what may appear to outsiders as a cowardly choice and leave evil to take its course.

Let us see how the revolutionaries and ambitious self-seekers of today, who proclaim that they want only justice, in fact pursue their aims.

A key factor here is universal education. Many more people are now able to read, write and express their opinions than could do so in the past. A vast number of new causes are espoused and pressure groups abound. It is impossible for the heads of governments, even if they were to work 24 hours a day, to listen to every faction. Nor can they delegate authority too freely because subordinates, by making mutually inconsistent decisions, might throw the system into chaos. Democracy, based upon free discussion and majority decision, is ill-equipped to deal with a babel of voices.

Frustration is the result: the inevitable result. Democracy is too slow to bring about reforms. The dedicated man knows he must be patient . . . yes . . . but for how long? . . . 'Till after he is dead? . . . Is there no quicker way? . . . When frustrations are voiced the revolutionary sees his chance.

In many parts of the world revolutionaries have developed a technique in the present century which, often modified to suit local conditions, has proved surprisingly effective. A group of men get together and decide to support a cause with a broad enough appeal to enlist widespread sympathy. First they enlist those who are already frustrated. The news is spread abroad that despite many efforts the normal democratic process has accomplished nothing. 'The people must be shown that social wrongs are not going to be redressed by civil means alone' (Che Guevara). If no such cause can be found, one is invented: Frank Kitson (*Gangs and Counter Gangs*, 1971) mentions several cases in which this was done.

People are urged to come out into the streets in as large numbers as possible so that the authorities will be made aware of their complaints. Processions, protest meetings and deputations are organized.

However, from the very start of the movement

the promoters plan confrontation with the police. 'It is desirable to have the oppressor, wittingly or not, break the peace first' says Che Guevara. If the authorities will not 'play' a few people can be deputed, if necessary paid, to start trouble. They may block a road, do physical damage to buildings, or throw stones at the police. Sooner or later the police are forced to react with force and to make arrests . . . Tempers are frayed . . . There are more arrests and more protests while violence grows apace. Eventually the military are called in, which is just what the revolutionaries want, for young trigger-happy soldiers sometimes fire into crowds.

The undeniable brutality of the authorities now provides a rallying point. The authorities have proved by their actions that they are unfit to govern. In their frantic efforts to keep the peace they conduct searches and make arrests. The people are made to feel that they need protection from endless interference in their way of life by police and soldiers.

The revolutionaries themselves now begin to play the role of protectors of the people. They murder police, soldiers, political VIPs and representatives of law and justice in revenge for what they, the authorities, have done. Inevitably the authorities react with yet more violence: interference in the lives of innocent people proceeds apace. Hatred of the authority increases and increasingly the population gives its support, at least passively, to its self-oppointed protectors. To many it seems that things could not be much worse any way: so in fairness and for the good of all, why not let the revolutionaries have a taste of power?

In all this the teaching of religion is ignored. The authorities are judged wicked and ruthless while the faults in those who seek to overthrow them are minimized, or even glamorized because they represent the poor, in violation of the principle laid down in the Bible: 'You shall not change your judgment according to whether your brother is rich or poor' (Lev. 19:15).

Following the procedure we have outlined, a very small group of men can often overthrow a government. In World War 1 Lawrence of Arabia used these methods against the Turks. In Cuba, Castro and Guevara were at one time down to twelve men but managed in the end to take over the whole country.

From the revolutionary's point of view this method has much to commend it. If men are determined at all costs to win a country over to communism, or to establish themselves as dictators, confrontation in the orthodox way will be dangerous and probably unsuccessful. Open clashes with troops, trained in the use of modern weapons, inevitably leads to defeat for insurgents. Invasion by the army of a neighbouring state might escalate and perhaps, in the end, start an atom war. The technique of subversion is altogether safer and more effective; the casualties, a few hundred or thousand at most, though regrettable, are much fewer than in open warfare.

How should a Christian view the scene? What ought he to do?

When subversion starts he will be told that as the organisers are fighting for the principle of justice, all good men have a duty to support the movement. It is the Christian's duty to love the down-trodden, to see that wrongs are put right. He should feel ashamed if he stays at home doing nothing while others give of their time to parade the streets with colourful banners.

Then what should the Christian decide to do? Shall he join in the general agitation? Or not? In an important book (*Violence*, 1970) Jacques Ellul discusses this question. He concludes that a Christian must not, cannot if he is faithful to his calling, join up with revolutionaries. For the demand for revolution and social justice comes from those who do not share Christian faith. These people want justice meted out to bad people, to the powerful, the rich, the capitalists, the Communists, the exploiters. But this is contrary to Christian faith. If God so loved the world that he gave his Son, he loves all men; not just the poor and weak, but the rich and powerful, the Neros, Hitlers, Himmlers as well as persecuted Jews, Christians and blacks. By siding with those who deny this, Christians forget their calling; they conform to the trend of the moment and in the end contribute nothing specifically Christian to the world.

In World War 2 many Christians joined the French resistance movement against the German occupiers: after D-day, says Ellul, 'I am bound to say that I saw no difference at all between the Nazi concentration camps and the camps in which France confined the collaborators.' Many Christians joined the national Liberation Front in the Algerian War. After the war they were 'utterly indifferent to the fate of those who were defeated'.

Professor Ellul paints a depressing historical picture of how generation after generation of Christians jump upon the band wagons of their day. Now they are linking up with socialism: yesterday it was liberalism, democracy, competitive capitalism, militaristic nationalism and in Germany even Nazism. For in Germany the German churches in the main accepted the values of the Nazi regime. Hitler was no coward. He exalted courage which appealed to Christians. He called the tune and many Christians gave their lives for him in battle. And today his methods are used throughout the world. He loosed the reign of violence: today it dominates the right and the left, the worlds of capitalism and of socialism. 'That violence is so generally condoned today shows that Hitler won his war after all: his enemies imitate him'. Today Christians participate in revolutionary violence just as fervently as they used to participate in military violence.

But what of the fight for justice? How are the wrongs of those who suffer injustly to be righted if Christians stand aloof?

The issue is complicated by three factors. If a Christian is satisfied that Christian principles are paramount in all three, it may be right for him to give what aid he can short of actual fighting.

Firstly the idea of justice is now associated in the minds of most people with the unChristian view that a man's life consists in the abundance of the things which he possesses. It is taken for granted that happiness is to be measured by consumption of goods, that the sole problem confronting our age is the unequal distribution of material wealth which can be rectified only by violence.

To foster violence the revolutionary socialists protest against paternalism, meaning that no self-respecting man wants to receive anything from a superior: he wishes rather to take it for himself by force.

No Christians can feel sympathy with this outlook. God's gifts do not come to us as a matter of right but of grace or unmerited kindness. If, though quite unworthy, we receive so much from God, we must be prepared not only to give freely but also to receive from our fellow men. There is nothing more devastating to character and to society at large (as H. Schöck has shown in his monumental book, *Envy: a Theory of Social Behaviour*, 1969) than the jealousy which arises because, when we receive, we tacitly admit the superiority of the giver and therefore envy him! Yet envy is seemingly encouraged by modern revolutionaries. Let us face them, then, with the question: If what you are fighting for could be obtained as a free-will gift and not as a matter of right from those who have it to give, would you accept it thankfully?

Secondly, what proof has the revolutionary to offer that he is interested in justice at all? Is his talk of justice the smoke screen behind which he seeks to achieve his own ambition or to promote his ideology? Suspicion is right, for the technique of revolution is now so well known.

A third point about which a Christian needs to be satisfied is this. How did the revolutionary movement come to choose the particular issue which they stress as their rallying ground?

Ellul reminds us that for every person murdered today whose cause is espoused by revolutionaries, ten more are murdered without any one to sponsor their cause or even to show interst.

Revolutionaries, including many Christians, today take up the cause of blacks in the USA and South Africas, or of the Palestinian Arabs, but for political reasons only. Over the past decade or two they have been quite unconcerned about the genocide of Indians in Brazil, the oppression of Tibetans by China, massacres of Kurds in Irak and Iran and of Christians in the Republic of Somali, or the fates of the monarchist Yemenites bombed, burned with napalm and even attacked with poison gas by Egypt in 1964–7, the attitude of Islamic governments towards minorities; the impoverishment of Kenyans occasioned by the exploitation of their land by those who grow crops for sale abroad; the misappropiation of foreign aid by governments (eg. Bangladesh) who use it to help the well-to-do rather than those who need it; the misery caused by the caste system in India . . . and so on . . . The reason is only too evident. To show concern about many evils is to invite political repercussions. Complain about Islamic cruelty and the supply of oil might stop! The political enemies of the revolutionaries would not be embarrassed if one of these other causes were taken up: something might sometimes be done to help the sufferers but it would not help the revolutionaries. Of course it is right for a Christian to help the oppressed, but in choosing whom to help, it is also right to give priority to those most in need and those whose cause is not sponsored by others.

7:
In conclusion

WHY HAS GOD called his people to be men of peace?

Not because violence is something alien to the nature of things. Far from it: the title of the BBC documentary 'The Violent Universe' was accurate enough. The creative 'Big Bang' of violence unimaginable, started the universe on its way: there has been violence ever since. On our puny earth we see it in flood, avalanche, lightning, hurricane, wave, earthquake and volcano: even in the cat catching the mouse. The very atoms of which we are made are the products of the violence of long ago. Our safety depends on the study of the ways and means of keeping violence at bay: we build dykes, locks and dams to prevent flooding and learn to 'pipe' dangerous high voltage electricity safely across the countryside. A thousand examples come to mind.

In addition to the violence there is also surpassing beauty and gentleness in nature. What sight more peaceful and beautiful than the setting sun, or the bow of promise in the sky, or the birds singing in the trees with the bees and butterflies below hard about their business, or the cat purring by the fire?

There is violence in nature but also tranquility and beauty, reminding us of human love and joy.

God created nature, so it is to be expected that nature and God will be alike in some respects at least. No analogy is perfect (the perfect analogy is an identity!) and because God is not nature the two differ in many ways. But one point they have in common is very plain: there is violence and gentleness in nature and there is violence and gentleness in God.

One big difference, however, is that the violence of God, as revealed in the Bible, is connected chiefly with sin, whereas this is not normally so in nature. Even so, in so far as man is concerned, there is a connection. If we ignore nature's laws, violence follows. We cannot safely eat poisons because they look nice, or walk on water, or ignore safety rules at work. Nor can we ignore God's laws and escape the violence ('the wrath' as Paul calls it) of God.

That God is a God both of violence and of gentleness and love is a fact we encounter all through the Bible. In Eden God walked with Adam in the cool of the evening but not long after a flaming sword was there to guard the way to the Tree of Life. God chose to reveal the Law at a mountain belching fire and smoke near which the quaking earth opened and swallowed men: it was here that he revealed himself as one 'showing steadfast love to thousands of those who love me and keep my commandments' (Ex. 20:5).

In the New Testament Jesus speaks often of the love of God but also of hell (gehenna) and of the day of judgment. St. Paul, writer of the beautiful hymn about love (1 Cor. 13) speaks also of the day when the enemies of Jesus 'shall suffer the punishment of eternal destruction' (2 Thess. 1:9). At the end of the Bible the Book of Revelation again tells us much about God's love but also about the violence of God which will destroy his enemies. Whether we like it or not, a combination of violence and gentleness is the way things are. It is seen in the Bible: it is seen in nature.

So much for the facts. How does man's duty come into the story? How far are we entitled to play the double role of nature – and of God?

At one time when men thought themselves righteous they were permitted (because of their hardness of heart, or insensitiveness to moral issues) to join forces with God in executing judgment on their fellow men. In this way we can understand the crusade wars of the Israelites in ancient times.

The Christian gospel, however, changes this. Faced with the devastating fact of goodness, seen in Jesus, man realizes at long last that every human being has sinned against God (Rom. 3). The Pharisee (not every Pharisee, of course) who represents the old order, recounts his virtues and thanks God that he is not as other men: the tax gatherer, approved by Jesus and representing the new order, dare not raise his eyes to heaven but says only 'God be merciful to me, a sinner!' (Lk. 18:13).

As Christians we are acutely conscious of having sinned. We are deeply sorry; we can only ask for the forgiveness and mercy which according to the thril-

103

ling Christian good news (gospel) is given freely to those who repent. But this being so, we are in no position to attack others, sword in hand, on the ground that they too, like us, have done wrong! We cannot do this because it puts us in the position of the slave in the gospels who owed his master an enormous sum of money but after being forgiven promptly threatened and imprisoned a fellow slave who owed him a few pence (Mt. 18:23f). Even when circumstances are against us and force seems the only way out, violence is still wrong – wrong for us but not for God. 'Vengeance is mine, I will repay says the Lord' (Rom. 12:19). Only those without sin can afford to throw stones at sinners (Jn. 8:7).

Often, of course, a Christian may be powerless against the wrongs that he sees. But if he has the opportunity he may find it possible to appeal to those at the top of the political ladder directly, and even tell them bluntly that they are doing wrong. Though it cost him his life, John the Baptist fearlessly told king Herod that his marriage to Herodias, his brother Phillip's wife, was sinful (Mt. ch.14 etc.). He must have said this openly but with no thought of rebellion.

We have seen how this lesson is taught again and again in the New Testament. What cause could have been more worthy, humanly speaking, than that which Peter espoused when he tried to prevent the capture of Jesus by his would-be murderers? Or the cause of the Christians in the last day who wish to fight the Antichrist, the incarnation of all that is evil? Yet it is in these two contexts, and these only, that the words 'They that take the sword shall perish by the sword' (Rev. 13:10) are found in the New Testament.

Christ's rule that we should not take the sword is clear enough, but it is nearly always possible to imagine circumstances in which it seems right to break a rule. We accept cannibalism as wrong, but Christians (the Pope included) did not condemn the party lost and ice-bound high on the Andes after an air crash for keeping alive by eating their dead companions when no other food of any kind was available for two entire months. (The story is told by E. H. Lopez in *The Highest Hell*, 1973.) We accept lying as wrong but it is easy to think of situations in which it seems right (to protect a friend a man might confess to a crime he did not commit). Stealing is wrong but it might be right to steal the gun of a would-be murderer, or the cyanide belonging to a would-be suicide. In the Bible the eating of consecrated bread was wrong save for priests only, but David and his men ate of it and were blameless. Similarly 'the priests in the temple profane the sabbath and are guiltless' (Mt. 12:3–5). God's commands are made for man's benefit, they are not straight jackets into which men must perforce be made to fit. 'The Sabbath was made for man, and not man for the Sabbath' (Mk. 2:27).

The important point is that it can never be right to use exceptions to moral principles as excuses for wholesale disregard of them. The man who thinks it right to tell his aged mother that she is not suffering from cancer when he knows that she is, must not take this as an excuse for persistent lying to his business partners even if he reckons that his lies will ultimately do good by destroying the reputations of those partners who are dishonest. The man who steals the potential suicide's poison must not raid chemists' shops, even if he thinks he can distribute drugs on a fairer basis than does the establishment.

In the same way it is possible to imagine a situation in which killing another human being might be right. Suppose, for instance, that I see a man about to throw a grenade into a bus or plane filled with people and that I have the opportunity to kill him first and prevent the disaster. Many committed Christians, opposed to war and violence on principle, might choose the 'lesser evil' in such a case. Again, anger is normally wrong, but in certain situations (cruelty to a child, or an animal) it would be right. But again it must be short lived. Rare moments of violence or anger do not warrant making them into a way of life. 'Be ye angry and do not sin; do not let the sun go down on your anger' (Eph. 4:26). In emergencies we may, indeed, be tempted to sin but the believing Christian will remember the promise: 'God is faithful, and he will not let you be tempted beyond your strength but with the temptation will also provide the way of escape' (1 Cor. 10:13).

The point that what we do in emergencies must be enacted quickly and done with is important. In a traditional war each side will claim to be peace loving and sincere: it is the other side that has done something wrong, so creating an emergency situation in which declaration of war is the only honourable course left open. People are told that the war situation is like the emergency situation in private life. Even the pacifist Christian might push a man, about to throw a bomb, off a moving bus and so kill him. The Christian nation ought to act in a basically similar manner towards a foreign nation committing, or about to commit, a wicked act. And the revolutionary will make out a similar case.

Faced with an argument presented along these lines tens of thousands who, in the normal way, are peacefully inclined will forget their scruples and join armies or guerrilla groups. In the end the distinction between Christian and non-Christian simply disappears: both sides become increasingly cruel and true religion is forgotten – save perhaps that each side may pray for victory.

What is wrong with the argument? It is, surely, that in an emergency we are not judging someone else because we think he is doing wrong: we are seeking to remedy a situation. We may react quickly and spontaneously in the only effective way we can: we do not sit down first and ask if the other fellow is a sinner and whether, suppose we decide he is, he ought to be punished.

In a traditional war, and in the present wars in which revolutionaries are engaged, this is however exactly what is done. The wicked Kaiser, ignoring his treaties, marched into Belgium: Hitler did the same in Poland. These actions were flagrant violations of international law. In Ireland the supposedly wicked police and soldiers kill people in the streets, search and disorder innocent peoples' houses and lock people up – Flagrant violations of justice! So once again it is a Christian duty to fight those who do these wrongs. Such are the thoughts of the non-pacifist Christian who engages in war or street fighting.

This argument against Christian pacifism will only appear plausible to those who forget the Lord's warning against judging others. Consciously, or unconsciously, it is easy at the back of our minds to imagine that it is our job, even our duty, to police the world. This belief is born of pride. It is fostered by imperial tradition, by extreme right wing politicians but also by some well known Christian movements. It is strengthened by carefully selected propaganda, at every time of crisis. In 1914, for instance, the stress was on the wickedness of the Germans who had marched into nearly defenceless Belgium: no one was reminded of the wickedness of the Belgiums who had slaughtered and enslaved Africans by the million in the Belgium Congo, or of the wickedness of the British who, by unprovoked war, had forced the Chinese to buy British opium. If it is right to argue from personal emergencies to national ones, then let us apply our Lord's words 'He that is without sin . . . let him first cast a stone' (Jn. 8:7) to national and group situations also. We need to remember what Jesus himself said when asked to adjudicate in a manifest case of unfairness: 'Who made me a ruler or divider over you?' (Lk. 12:14). God is the judge: 'Vengeance is mine, I will repay' (Heb. 10:30 etc).

This teaching of the New Testament is being forgotten by many Christians today, especially in Latin America. Christians, mostly Roman Catholic priests (though without Papal approval) are arguing that it is their job and that of the church to organise rebellion against corrupt governments, their job to bring down the mighty from their seat, exalt the lowly and set the prisoner free. (See for example L. Boff, *Jesus Christ: Liberator*, SPCK, 1980 – the literature is extensive).

Such teaching is a denial of what the Bible tells us. We have seen how corrupt governments gain power in our day. But it is the revolutionaries and the common people, often aided by Christians, who put them in power. It is the people who parade the streets, who encourage agitation and who, in the end, allow revolutionaries to take over. Corrupt forms of government are in large measure a judgment of God. This is the clear teaching of the story of the establishment of the monarchy in Israel in the Old Testament (1 Sam. Ch. 8). The Israelites demanded a king and God was displeased: 'They have rejected me from being king over them.' (v. 7) Nevertheless they persisted. God, speaking through the prophet Samuel, told them what the result would be: 'In that day you will cry out because of your king, whom you have chosen for yourselves; but the Lord will not answer you' (v. 18). In short the sufferings which Israel later endured because of the monarchy were in part a punishment for their sin in demanding a king. They had been warned. In the same way those who encourage and enable revolutionaries to take over governments today have but themselves to blame when things go wrong. The governments they choose are part of the judgment of God.

Today self-defence, or defence of home and country, looms large as one of the factors which prevents the acceptance of Christian pacifism. Let us see why this seems so important at the present time.

Increasingly widespread use of computers and the utilisation of robots which work in factories untiringly for 24 hours a day and need little supervision, are bound to increase unemployment in the Western world. Science and technology have enormously increased the productivity of those in work – even on the farm the land yields much more food than formerly. In addition the modern world is waking up to the fact that natural resources will not last for ever: soon it will no longer make sense to produce cars which rust away in a year or two or furniture which the children will break. Things will have to be made to last and this again must reduce employment.

By and large in the Western world most people have all that they need. To increase demand (and so employment, and profits) manufacturers advertise that greed is need – the new luxury car is positively needed to take the children to school, the colour television is as necessary as furniture and holidays in far away lands are near essential for refreshment of mind and body. Such tactics increase employment but there are limits to stimulating demand in this way. The net cumulative effect of modern development is increased unemployment.

The easiest way to increase employment, as Hitler found in the 1930s, is to make armaments. They call for high level skills which keep potentially dangerous academics contented and their overall use of raw materials is not great (quite modest in communication technology: after battles, as in the near East, the metal dealers soon remove tanks and guns for recycling). The arms industry is well calculated to shorten the dole queues. But the making of weapons is immoral and dangerous. They are a threat to potential enemies and these include Christians in other lands who, as in Russia, have suffered enough for their faith. How then can a government justify the possession of a large and powerful arms industry? Only, surely, by claiming that in addition to maintaining employment, it is necessary for defence. In this way the most hideous of all modern developments – the making and deployment of atomic weapons, the so-called deterrent – is defended.

The simple Christian does not know the answer to all the world's problems. He does not know how to deal with the unemployment issue. He knows however, that like others, he is vulnerable. But he can at least see that present dangers are great and that the policies adopted are wrong. What would he think of two personal enemies if they filled their mansions with booby traps, guns and explosives just in case they were unexpectedly attacked? For that is the way the nations behave. If we follow Christ we have no right to think of our defence in such terms. Is it not obvious that if ever we are invaded, co-operation and kindness shown to the enemy would prove a vastly safer policy than the launching of missiles? Who would benefit by the creation of atomic wastelands where once cities thrived and farmers grew food for mankind? One does not have to be a Christian pacifist to see the wickedness of retaliating in such a way.

The main issues about Christian teaching on violence now seem clear enough. But how far should such ideas be applied today? Here several questions may be asked.

Firstly, how can a pacifist position be squared with a Christian's position in society? The safety of us all depends upon the work of the police, but the police use violence against the criminal. Does not the very fact that we are citizens compromise us with violence?

Some Christians, Ellul among them, think that it does. They urge us to remember that if we use violence we must remember its laws: the law of the slipery slope of compromise which will make it hard to stop before we have gone too far; the law of reciprocity, that those who take the sword will be killed with the sword, and the law that violence sows seeds of hatred. If we believe that by the very nature of society we are in some degree guilty of violence, then we must resolve to be as near faithful to God as humanly possible. 'If possible, as far as it depends upon you, live peacefully with all men' (Rom. 12:18) as St. Paul puts it.

Many early Christians must have felt the same dilemmas as we do. They were commanded by Christ to render to Caesar what was Caesar's and by Paul too, to pay the taxes that were due (Rom. 13:6–7) but the money must often have been used in

112

ways of which Christians deeply disapproved. Were they guilty because they helped to pay for what was done? Surely not! But the Christians benefitted from the *pax Romana* yet were not prepared to fight for the empire to maintain the peace. Was not this hypocritical?

The objection might be answered in several ways. Early Christians would have said that the criticism assumes that we must put loyalty to our fellow men, or to the State, above loyalty to God. We receive many things from God: shall we show our ingratitude by doing willfully what he has told us not to do? If it is a question of being disloyal, or seemingly disloyal to our fellow men, or to God, we ought to give God the priority.

Coming nearer to our own times, there is an obvious parallel with the days of slavery when it was almost impossible to live in England without, at least in some measure, benefitting from slave labour. We have quoted the criticism that a man could hardly enquire into the pedigree of every chair on which he sat! It was impossible, at that time, to live (unless one went out into the fields to eat berries) as an opponent of slavery without in some measure 'hypocritically' benefitting from slavery. Similarly, today, many believe that violence is wrong, yet willy nilly they must accept the protection afforded by the State. Therefore they are hypocrites – or so it might be argued.

But is not the logic being pushed too far? Perhaps those who use such arguments are more hypocritical than those they criticise, for criticism of this kind tends to stifle reforms of every kind. One of our ancestors might have said: 'The Church in her wisdom persecutes witches and I receive benefit since they are dead who would otherwise cast their evil spells upon me: so what right have I to criticise witchhunting?' If I claim that I wish only to do good to my fellow man and use arguments against others which effectively paralyse reforms, am I not a hypocrite?

Even so, not every conscience will be satisfied by rebutting the argument. We have seen how in the 4th and 5th centuries thousands of Christians left their homes and cities and went to live as hermits in the desert. Nor was the gesture futile. Multitudes flocked to the deserts to hear the word of God. St. Simeon Stylites (390–459 AD) who lived on a pillar, commanded a prominent ruler to countermand the order to destroy Jewish synagogues and was obeyed. Quite possibly, in our day too, God may call some of his people to do strange things. If so, who are we to judge?

Ellul very rightly points out that some Christians in high position, receiving more than their fair share of worldly goods, will feel that by doing so they are acting violently towards the poor. Such people should spend what money they need to live in a modest way, says Ellul, and give the rest of their income away.

St. Paul's advice about food offered to idols also provides us with a valuable guide (1 Cor. 8). In some parts of the Roman Empire a Christian who on principle avoided all food offered to idols might have been very hungry. Paul's answer is not that he should starve, but that he should eat food set before him with thankfulness to God. If, however, he found that by so doing offence was caused, he should stop eating food known to have been offered to idols. In the same way we too can accept the protection offered us in the normal way, giving thanks to God. But if individuals are involved who might be harmed by this attitude, we must be prepared to suffer, if needs be becoming 'extremists' with them, lest we cause offence.

By now it is surely clear that violence and threats of violence have become the sin of our age. Imagine almost any one of the true Christians who lived and died before say, 1900, rising from the dead and viewing the modern scene. Suppose we ask him what he thinks of the ways we conduct our wars – civil as well as national. Is it likely that we shall find a single one who would condone what we condone today, who will tell us that it is right for a Christian to join guerrilla forces or the forces of his nation or learn, even in times of peace, to use the hideously cruel weapons that we have invented? Many of those long since dead thought it right on occasion to fight in just wars, but certainly they would not reckon our wars are just.

These Christians of the past were horrified by the new weapons of their day – improved bows and arrows, squibs to frighten horses, gunpowder to tear men to pieces in fiery death, or canon balls to hit men unawares breaking their bones. What would they think of torpedoing a ship, dropping a bomb on a town, burning men and women with jellified petrol or phosphorus incendiaries? What would they think of those who plant a bomb in a public place and run away hoping that the murder and mutilation of innocent victims will draw attention to some real or imaginary injustice? What would they think of a so-called Christian country which harbours missiles on its territory, ready aimed at far away cities and able at a few minute's notice to kill thousands, perhaps hundreds of thousands, of fellow human beings in atomic holocausts?

We Christians of the 20th century are one with the Church triumphant. We deplore the cruelties of former generations who revered the name of Christ. If we had lived in their day we should not have joined in the blood-thirsty Crusades, or tormented women supposed to be guilty of witchcraft, or bought and sold slaves, or persecuted to the death those whose theological opinions differed from those of the establishment. But were their sins greater than ours? We in the Christian West have taught the world the devilish arts of scientific warfare. The undeveloped countries buy our tanks, our guns, our fighter planes, our missiles, and receive training in their use from us.

The point must have come home to many when, in 1974, the Turkish government decided to permit once again the cultivation of the opium poppy. The USA government protested strongly on the ground that, despite Turkish intentions to prevent export of opium, much of it was certain to reach American shores where it would ruin the lives of many young Americans. The Turkish government replied that by that agrument the USA should stop making guns because 100,000 of them reached Turkey every year. The fact is that the West (and Russia too) distributes its devilish wares throughout the world and thinks that it has a right to do so. It may well be that many Christians are engaged in their manufacture and certainly it is rare for Christians to protest.

Why has Christianity changed so much from the religion of gentleness that once it was, the religion that seeks to overcome evil by good? It is the old story; once we compromise with sin there is no safeguard against further and yet further compromise. The only way back is the way of repentance and repentance must start with the individual.

Finally, it is often said that Christianity is too idealistic to be practical. The point is taken, yet the Christian gospel still has power to change lives. Suppose, however, we agree that our Lord's teaching about non-resistance to the evil man rarely works. What then does the ciritic propose to put in its place?

Both in national wars and now in subversion followed by violence, mankind is learning that retaliation with violence is no more likely to prove successful than the non-violent way of Jesus.

Everyone now realises that the stockpiling of weapons as a safeguard against national war is exceedingly dangerous, the more so as more nations join the nuclear club. Present policies must mean that in the end, whether by accident or design, a bomb will explode . . . And then? . . . The very existence of great stocks of fissile material – enough to kill every soul on earth many times over – is an open invitation to insurgents everywhere to steal some of it: already enough has unaccountably disappeared to make many bombs. With fissile material available the construction of a bomb in a back garden is not too difficult an undertaking according to the experts, and blackmail is a frightening possibility . . . Can any one seriously claim that, even at the political level, present policies of so-called Christian nations are less dangerous than Christian pacifism?

However, Christianity is not, and was never intended to be, a worldly religion. The Christian desires, above all else, to love, serve and glorify God: love of his neighbour takes a second (though vastly important) place. In the beautiful New Testament imagery, the church is the bride of Christ. Our job is to build up beautiful character, both in ourselves and in others. 'His bride has made herself ready' (Rev. 19:7).

Appendix

Note on Romans 13:1–7

THIS PASSAGE IS often cited by non-pacifist Christians as the main scriptural ground for their position. So let us see what Paul says.

St. Paul starts by urging Christians to be 'subject to the governing authorities'. (In this brief sentence he does not refer to the possibility of a clash between the commands of God and the commands of men, but, had he digressed on the subject, it is inconceivable that he would have put man above God.) The reason given for subjection is that 'there is no authority except from God, and those (authorities) that exist have been instituted by God. Therefore he who resists the authorities resists what God has appointed'.

Here it seems that Paul has in mind the Jewish-Christian view of Providence. The world is God's. He is in control. He raises up governments and men to work out his purposes, whether of beneficence or of judgment for sin.

In the Bible those who did wicked deeds, even, were often unknowingly servants or ministers of

God. Joseph's brothers sold him into Egypt but Joseph says, 'God sent me before you to preserve life . . .it was not you who sent me here but God' (Gen. 45:5, 8). Pharoah was raised up expressly to carry out God's will (Rom. 9:17). Nebuchadnezzar who knew nothing of God was nevertheless God's servant (Jer. 25:9; 27:6). Of the foreign king Cyrus it is written, 'He is my shepherd, and he shall fulfil all my purposes' (Is. 44:28) and again, Cyrus was God's 'annointed . . . I call you by your name . . . though you do not know me' (Is. 45:1, 4). Ahasuerus (Esth.) and others in the Old Testament were God's servants or ministers in this sense. They were raised up 'for the sake of my servant Jacob, and Israel my chosen' (Is. 45:4).

Paul applies the same thinking to the Christian community. The Roman ruler was God's minister, punishing crime and making the existence of the infant church possible. On one occasion at least Paul owed his life to Roman soldiers when his countrymen had vowed to murder him (Acts 23).

Paul next rewords the point he has just made, making his language still more emphatic. Secular powers are ordained of God and are not to be opposed because (in general) they approve good works and are armed with the sword to execute 'wrath on the wrong doer'. The church benefits greatly from this state of affairs: the state, therefore, 'is God's servant for your good' while those whose work it is to collect taxes 'are ministers of God'. So Christians must pay taxes (compare our Lord's 'render to Caesar the things that are Caesar's . . .') and must show respect and honour where it is due.

This teaching is simple and clear. It follows directly after the close of Chapter 12 which is virtually a summary of the Sermon on the Mount ('If your enemy is hungry feed him . . . Overcome evil with good' etc). It seems inconceivable that otherwise fairminded expositors of the Bible should sometimes forget the context of Romans 13 and argue that because the state is organised by 'servants of God' (13:4) Christians should on occasion be prepared to obey the State rather than Jesus. Yet the argument is often encouraged. As well might one, if so commanded, emulate the wrong doings of other 'servants of God', such as Joseph's brothers, Pharoah or Nebuchadnezzar.

Early Christians understood clearly enough that they were called to obey God rather than men. Only in later times when ideas and practices alien to Paul's day had become established, did Christians begin to amplify the passage and to read into it situations that were not there at the beginning.

(1) In Paul's day there was but one central government and, except for occasional skirmishes at the frontiers of the Roman Empire, there was peace. The age of separate sovereign states was not yet. The passage says nothing about the duty of a Christian towards a sovereign state other than his own in peace or war.

(2) Christians in Paul's day were a tiny minority of the population, mostly of the slave class. They neither participated in government nor ever expected to. They were told to be subject to the government. The situation of later times when Christian princes were themselves rulers must not

be read into the passage.

(3) Democracy in its modern sense had not come on the scene. In a democracy obedience to the power is obedience to the will of the majority. Christians, like others, have a right to win others to their point of view and to change the government. No such possibility existed in Paul's day.

How should Paul's teaching be applied today? A common argument is that since the state is God's servant, Christians should be prepared to support it and to participate in wielding power. Since, it is ordained of God, the state, 'is the servant of God to execute his wrath (or vengeance, as in 13:9) on the wrongdoer' (v. 4), therefore Christians too, in the service of the state, must be prepared to take the sword, and fight in wars when so required.

As we have noted, there is nothing at all of all this in the passage as its stands. At a stretch the passage might be used to justify the Christian who helps the state to fight the criminal, but it gives no support to war.

Very much the reverse! 'There is no authority except from God and those that exist have been instituted by God' (v. 1). This can only mean that any country which uses its powers to organise society and to fight crime is instituted by God. To oppose such a government, (our own or any other government), says Paul, is to oppose God. 'He who resists the authorities resists what God has appointed, and those who resist will incur judgment'.

Could words express the Christian pacifist position more forcefully? If we fight another nation with its system of rewards and punishments, we fight against what God has ordained and we shall incur God's judgment.

The passage has greatly troubled later generations. Would Paul have written as he did in a time of insurrection when no one quite knew which power group would win the day? Or in Nazi Germany? (But were the Nazis worse than the Romans with their gladiatorial shows, mass crucifixions and public burnings of Christians as by Nero?). We do not know. Certainly his words, 'If possible, as far as it depends upon you, live peaceably with all' would still have stood. Christians have debated the subject endlessly: here we are only concerned with what the Bible, as it stands, says about Christian pacifism.

Brief summary

In *Chapter 1* we saw how, over the centuries, each new weapon used in war seemed horrible to contemporaries. But sooner or later it was taken for granted until a new horror shocked mankind. This and many another development suffered the same fate. In compromising with what they know to be wrong men, including Christians, step on a slippery slope. Thereafter they cannot say 'Thus far but no farther' for there is no stable foothold. With the advent of nuclear weapons man has now slipped so far that the final plunge down the precipice cannot be for long delayed – humanly speaking.

In *Chapter 2* we thought of some of the evils that have been committed by otherwise humane people who were often Christians. Some of these are so terrible that we need to ask how men came to act as they did. The New Testament has much to say about (1) the numbing of the conscience, (2) the effects of fear (in the sense of dread) as when, in the past, Europe was terrified by the imaginary plots which witches were thought to be hatching; and (3) the notion that some people are less than fully human – here we considered the difficulty of breaking away from convention as in the days when it was reckoned respectable and right to participate in the slave trade.

In *Chapter 3* we examined what the Old Testament says about war. We found that what was permitted, or commanded, in the wars of ancient Israel, and what is accepted today in modern war, differ so greatly that the one cannot possibly be used to justify the other. The wars of the Old Testament were not, for example, national at all: an Israelite might be called upon to fight a neighbouring city in his own country if those who lived there had forgotten the Law of the Lord. But the Old Testament contains many hints that war is not the best that God has in mind for man.

In *Chapter 4* we examined the teaching of the New Testament about war. We found that in the Sermon on the Mount, where Jesus said 'Love your enemies', he meant (or at least included) the national enemy. The attempt to make his words apply only (or even mainly) to private enemies destroys the contrast ('it was said . . . but I say unto you) to which he repeatedly drew attention. Many other passages confirmed the view that for a Christian participation in war is sinful.

In *Chapter 5* we asked how early Christian interpreted New Testament teaching concerning violence. In peace time the Roman army acted effectively like the civil service of today and soldiers might see nothing of fighting over several generations. But if called upon to fight Christians were normally expected to resign immediately from the army. Sometimes refusal to fight led to martyrdom: a few such martyrs were canonized in later times, in marked approval of the stand they took.

In *Chapter 6* we examined the tactics of those who, today, realising how dangerous and foolish the use of force against a well-trained army equipped with modern weapons would be, resort to subversion and revolution. We saw how wrong-headed and hypocritical it is for a Christian to join their ranks.

In *Chapter 7* we saw that God, like nature which is his creation, is a God of power and justice as well as of love, but that in their dealings with their fellowmen Christians are called upon to show God's love only, not his justice. Nevertheless, in rare moments, we may need to act quickly and decisively to avoid evil. The biblical teaching is that acts of this kind, which have an outward appearance of imitating God's justice must not be prolonged: if we feel anger, even, it must be finished with before we sleep at night. Calculated plans on how best to beat an enemy are alien to the Gospel: they imply the judgment of others as if God had appointed us to be their judges.

We then turned to the defence argument and noted the reasons why it is pressed so strongly at the present time. Neither this, nor the political view of Christianity, which flourishes in some countries today, make sense in the light of Christian teaching. With St. Paul we must accept the fact that the political powers in the world are ordained by God — sometimes they are sent as judgments. The Christian must not oppose them physically; the only weapons available to him are the weapons of love and understanding.

Index

128

130